Extraordinary Ministry
in Ordinary Time

Extraordinary Ministry in Ordinary Time

An Invitation to Renewal for Pastors

James A. Harnish

UPPER
ROOM BOOKS®
NASHVILLE

Cover design: Micah Kandros | micahkandrosdesign.com
Interior design and typesetting: PerfecType | Nashville, TN

Print ISBN: 978-0-8358-1912-1 | Mobi ISBN: 978-0-8358-1913-8 | Epub ISBN: 978-0-8358-1914-5

If we are to follow Christ, it must be in our
common way of spending every day.
—William Law (1686–1761)

With gratitude for the United Methodist congregations in Florida that received me as their pastor and with whom I shared the long and joyful obedience.

Trinity, DeLand (1972–1975)
Howe Memorial, Crescent City (1975–1979)
St. Luke's, Orlando (1979–1992)
Hyde Park, Tampa (1992–2014)
First Church, Orlando (2018)

I thank my God every time I remember you, constantly praying with joy in every one of my prayers for all of you, because of your sharing in the gospel from the first day until now. I am confident of this, that the one who began a good work among you will bring it to completion by the day of Jesus Christ.

—Philippians 1:3-6, NRSV

CONTENTS

INTRODUCTION

*O*rdinary. The adjective reeks with the scent of stale sameness, the bitter whiff of bland boredom, the sour odor of lifeless order. It leaves a faint aroma of unexceptional drudgery in doing the same old things in the same old way without a hint of newness or a trace of creativity.

Who really wants to be ordinary?

According to the Enneagram personality types, I'm a Type 4 Individualist. That means I tend to see myself as being unique or different. It also means that I want the things around me to be distinctive or special. Type 4s are almost genetically resistant to being ordinary. My aversion to the word only strengthened when I learned that in British tradition the noun *ordinary* refers to a clergyperson who walks with a condemned prisoner on the way to death. Who would want to do the work if that's what it looks like to be an ordinary pastor?

And then there is Ordinary Time. It's the longest season in the liturgical year, beginning on the first Sunday after Pentecost (Trinity Sunday) and ending on Reign of Christ (also called Christ the King) Sunday, the last Sunday before the beginning of the new church year in Advent. The high holy days of Lent and Easter and The Great Fifty Days leading to Pentecost are behind us. Stretching through the dog days of summer in the Northern Hemisphere, most of the Sundays are designated simply in numerical order: "The _____ Sunday after Pentecost." Just another ordinary Sunday in Ordinary Time.

Who wants to be an ordinary pastor living in Ordinary Time? But then the disturbing truth settles upon us. Ordinary Time is where we practice most of our ministry. Every week isn't Holy Week, and every Sunday isn't Easter. Sooner or later, every person

11

called into Christian ministry discovers something that lay disciples learn just about every day. High, holy moments alive with spiritual exhilaration are the exception. Most of us invest most of our days in the ordinary stuff of ordinary life. Whether we thrive or merely survive depends on what we do with the ordinary days.

This book is my invitation to pastors and other people in ministry along with the lay people who serve with them to use what the liturgical calendar calls Ordinary Time as a metaphor for the ordinary days of ministry. It's an invitation

- for people who are beginning their ministry to develop patterns of spiritual discipline that will sustain them along the way;
- for people who are midway through their career to renew their calling and reenergize their passion;
- for people who are nearing the end of their ministry to reflect on what they have experienced in order to prepare for a new chapter ahead; and
- for lay men and women to grow in their understanding of and support for their pastors by sharing in prayer and reflection with them.

In an interview shortly after he completed his paraphrase of the New Testament called *The Message,* Eugene H. Peterson said that while he was doing the hard work of translation, he had a sense that it was "harvest time. This is the fruit of everything I've been doing already."[1] This book is, in a sense, the harvest of what I've been doing across more than four decades of pastoral ministry in United Methodist congregations in Florida. My appointments included a university town, a rural community, a new congregation in a rapidly growing suburb, and a historic church in an urban center. The spiritual soil in which the book grew was tilled and fertilized by clergy and laypersons who mentored, encouraged, challenged, and frustrated me along the way. My soul-level desire is to help people in ministry develop spiritual disciplines and personal relationships that will enable them to experience the joy that I have experienced in the long obedience of pastoral ministry.

My experience has confirmed that the most effective way to nourish our souls is not to depend on extraordinary moments of spiritual inspiration or dramatic changes in the patterns of our life. Instead, the foundation of spiritual nourishment is practicing the ordinary, time-tested disciplines of reflection on scripture, spiritual reading, prayer combined with what John Wesley called "spiritual conversation" with trusted friends in Christian community, and self-giving service to others. Our ministries depend upon what we do with our ordinary time in ordinary places.

"Ordinary time" can also represent a "fallow season" in our lives and ministries. I was going through one of those fallow seasons in both my congregation and my own life when a farmer friend taught me that every field needs a fallow season. During such a season, the soil is plowed but left unplanted so the nutrients in the soil can be restored to be more productive in the future. Without a fallow season, the earth will become depleted and no longer able to produce healthy crops. When nothing appears to be happening, the soil actually is being replenished for a growth season ahead.

My friend challenged me to use my personal fallow season to dig deeper into the soil of my soul so the Spirit of God could prepare me for more productive days ahead. He taught me to use the fallow season in my congregation as a time to pause from our hyperactivity; a space for deeper reflection on our mission, our ministry, and our calling; a time to renew our sense of God's Spirit at work within us by looking for signs of new life in unexpected places. With the psalmist, I experienced the way the Holy Spirit "satisfied the one who was parched with thirst, and he filled up the hungry with good things!" (Ps. 107:9).

This six-week guide focuses on themes I have found critically important for my ministry in the ordinary days and the fallow seasons: power, people, place, proclamation, perseverance, and promise. The daily readings are designed to help us develop our custom-made practices of spiritual formation to sustain and strengthen our lives and ministries in the ordinary times.

Daily Scripture

The nonnegotiable witness of the Christian tradition is that genuine transformation is always rooted in living with scripture so that by the power of the Holy Spirit, the written Word becomes a living Word in and through us. In this process we enter into scripture not for information but for participation. We read the Word not in order to extract sermon points or abstract principles but to guide us into life-transforming behaviors. We read the Bible not simply to remember old stories from the past but to allow the "old, old story of Jesus and his love" to become our own story in the present, pointing us toward God's kingdom-shaped future. Some of the daily scripture readings in this resource come from Revised Common Lectionary readings for Ordinary Time.

Readings for Reflection

The daily reflections come from my pastoral experience and from the witness of others who have strengthened my faith and encouraged my ministry across the years. The good news is that we are not the first people to follow the path of Christian ministry. We walk along a way of obedience that others have walked before us. I'm grateful for preachers, poets, professors, and ordinary people whose words and lives continue to inspire my own discipleship. This resource also grows out of ongoing conversation with a diverse group of pastors who read the manuscript and offered observations along the way. Their insights, corrections, and questions combined with the careful eye of Martha, my wife and best editor, have kept my words connected to the ordinary life in which we experience the extraordinary presence of God.

Journaling

By today's standards, the early Methodists were neurotically methodical in keeping a journal of their spiritual progress. Richard

Heitzenrater took us into their practice when he discovered the diary of Benjamin Ingham, one of John Wesley's early followers at Oxford. Heitzenrater described the journal as "a Methodist's constant companion and conscience . . . a ledger of the soul and a mirror for the spirit, recording and reflecting the progress and pitfalls of his struggle to advance along the path of holy living."[2]

When I look at the journals that I have filled over the years, I doubt that I or anyone else will ever read them. I wrote my thoughts and prayers not for a later use but to give me clarity in the present and to focus my wandering attention in prayer. To encourage readers to develop their own pattern of journaling and prayer, each day in this guide includes questions to prompt personal reflections.

Meditation and Prayer

Because of the unique way the Holy Spirit touches our individual lives, no one can prescribe the specific pattern or style of prayer most appropriate for each of us. In the first half of the twentieth century, Harry Emerson Fosdick, the nationally known preacher at The Riverside Church in New York City, pointed out that Jesus "prayed as naturally as a child breathes."[3] He described the way Jesus prayed differently depending on the circumstances at different times.

For our praying to become as natural as our breathing, our patterns of prayer will necessarily be suited to our personality and the circumstances we face along the way. The critical factor is creating a pause in our busy lives to be in the presence of God, to deepen our walk with Christ, and to allow the Holy Spirit to be at work in us. Discovering our pattern for prayer is a little like becoming a jazz musician. The process begins with learning the basic chord structures and rhythms, which then allows each musician to become a creative artist as he or she improvises his or her tunes.

Small-Group Community

Wesley scholar Jack Jackson underscored John Wesley's conviction that "field preaching without a corresponding link to a smaller community where people could watch over one another in love was . . .

a waste of time."[4] While people were "awakened" in large, public gatherings, they were spiritually nurtured, encouraged, and held accountable for their discipleship in small groups. The extraordinary moments of spiritual inspiration and commitment were translated into the ordinary patterns of their lives in the "bands" and "class meetings."

Methodist preachers were bound together in what Mr. Wesley called the *connexion* (Wesley's spelling), or conference. I believe that the conference was relational before it was institutional. We catch the spirit of this *connexion* in Charles Wesley's hymn that is still sung at the opening of Methodist conferences around the globe.

And are we yet alive,
and see each other's face?
Glory and thanks to Jesus give
for his almighty grace!

What troubles have we seen,
what mighty conflicts past,
fightings without, and fears within,
since we assembled last!

Yet out of all the Lord
hath brought us by his love;
and still he doth his help afford,
and hides our life above. (UMH, no. 553)

One of the sustaining gifts to my ministry has been a small group of pastors who have shared life together for more than three decades. The laughter and tears, hopes and hurts, successes and failures of these brothers have sustained all of us in hope-filled and life-giving ways. I hope other ministers will share this resource in a small group of colleagues. The book also could be used in a group of laypersons that becomes a similar kind of *connexion* with their pastor. Suggestions for developing this kind of community and a small-group discussion guide appear at the end of the book.

May we begin our journey with the expectation that God's extraordinary love and grace will strengthen us for the long and joyful obedience of ministry.

Questions for Journaling

- What is your personal description of *ordinary time*?
- When have you experienced a fallow season in your life or ministry?
- What is your deepest need or hope as you begin this journey?

Prayer

Loving God, even as you entered into the ordinary places of human life in Jesus Christ, I pray that you will meet me in the ordinary times and places where I live and serve with your extraordinary love and grace. Renew, refresh, and reenergize my ministry by the presence and power of your Holy Spirit. I pray in the name and spirit of Jesus Christ, the living Lord. Amen.

Week 1   Power

Everybody needs redemptive assistance from outside—
from God, family, friends, ancestors . . . and exem-
plars. . . . You have to draw on something outside yourself
to cope with the forces inside yourself.

—David Brooks

List 3 people
who have helped you
"cope with the forces inside
yourself"

The Long Obedience

Read Philippians 3:1-21.

Where do we find the power to see us through the long obedience of our ministry? How do we draw upon the spiritual power that will keep us energized on the journey through ordinary time? One way is to remember how we got into this work in the first place.

Vesper Hill was one of the early stops along my journey. On this gently sloping, grass-covered hillside overlooking the rolling hills and farmland of central Pennsylvania, youth from summer camp would spread their blankets as they gathered for evening worship. With any luck I'd find a girl to share the blanket with me!

It was a simple service: a few familiar songs, a scripture reading, a message by one of the camp leaders, followed by a time of silence for meditation, prayer, or just looking at the sky. The service ended with the same song every evening. We would continue singing as we made our way back down the hill and into the camp. The song is so deeply imbedded in my memory that nearly six decades later I can still hear us singing:

> Follow, I will follow Thee, my Lord,
> Follow ev'ry passing day.[1]

The song promises that God knows all the tomorrows that are before us and will be there to lead us along the way.

As a preacher who would eventually preach in youth camp services, I confess that I don't remember a single word of a single sermon from any those vesper services. But I do remember that song. It was in moments like the ones on Vesper Hill when I started following Jesus, and I've been following him ever since. It was the place where I began the long obedience of God's call to ministry.

When I sang the words of assurance that God would lead me all the way, I never could have imagined where that way would take me: the people I'd meet, the places I'd go, the challenges I'd face, the opportunities I'd be given, the tears I'd shed, and the laughter I'd share. It's all been the unanticipated gift of "a long obedience in the same direction." That phrase comes from Friedrich Nietzsche, the German philosopher who in 1882 declared, "God is dead." Nietzsche was wrong about God, but he was right about this.

> The essential thing "in heaven and in earth" is . . . that there should be long obedience in the same direction, there thereby results, and has always resulted in the long run, something which has made life worth living.[2]

Nietzsche's words ring true in just about every area of life: The essential thing, the thing that really makes life worth living, is a long obedience in the same direction. It's true for anyone who follows Jesus Christ and is called to serve in Christian ministry. What makes the difference is a long, persistent, often stumbling, always imperfect obedience to the words, way, and will of Jesus Christ.

Paul describes that long obedience in his letter to the Philippians:

> It's not that I have already reached this goal or have already been perfected, but I pursue it, so that I may grab hold of it because Christ grabbed hold of me for just this purpose. Brothers and sisters, I myself don't think I've reached it, but I do this one thing: I forget about the things behind me and reach out for the things ahead of me. The goal I pursue is the prize of God's upward call in Christ Jesus. (3:12-14)

This long obedience will include critically important moments along the way—decisive moments when we choose to follow Christ in some new direction, formative moments when we are called to take the next step in our discipleship, discouraging moments when we are tempted to throw in the towel, painful moments that can make or break us. It will include twists and turns we never expected, and we will face times when we take a detour or have to turn around and go back to the place where we lost our sense of direction. There will be exhilarating moments when we know that this is the moment for which we were created. But over the long haul, the essential thing is continuing to follow Jesus one day at a time, from today to all our tomorrows. I remember a camp meeting preacher declaring it doesn't matter how high saints jump as long as they keep walking when they hit the ground.

But for some, the long obedience doesn't always work out that way. Demas is the case in point. We know very little about him. We know that he is with Paul during his imprisonment in Rome (see Colossians 4:14). In the letter to Philemon, Paul identifies him as a "coworker" (v. 24). Demas has responded to the invitation to follow Christ. He has heard God's call and has become a partner in ministry with Paul, even to the point of staying engaged with Paul while he is in prison. But something happens along the way. In his second letter to Timothy, Paul writes sadly, "Demas has fallen in love with the present world and has deserted me and has gone to Thessalonica" (4:10). The high moments of holy idealism have faded away. Demas is unable to hang in there for the long haul of ordinary time.

I've known folks like Demas. They are gifted, spiritually alive, faithful people who respond in obedience to God's call. They start out with high hopes and noble ideals. But something happens along the way. Sometimes it's a major disappointment or a moral failure. Sometimes it's an ethical compromise. Sometimes it's conflict with difficult church members. Sometimes it's simply the tedium of the ordinary stuff of ordinary pastoral life in ordinary places. Some leave the ministry as an act of integrity because they can no longer deal with the hypocrisy or ineffectiveness of the institutional church. Others may suffer a breakdown of spiritual discipline or be overwhelmed by the loneliness of doing ministry without a community of support and accountability around them.

I touched on the outer edges of that experience during a fallow season in my life and ministry. I was leading a rapidly growing church in the suburbs of Orlando, tucked in between Walt Disney World and Universal Studios. The creative energy of the place was infectious. Everything in the church was booming, but I felt worn out physically and spiritually. I remember the day I half-heartedly asked a friend in professional staffing at Disney World if he had a place for a former preacher. He laughed and said, "You have no idea how many preachers up north get close to retirement and think they are a perfect match for the Magic Kingdom!" He clearly thought I'd better stick with what I was doing rather than try to escape into Fantasy Land.

By contrast, I've also known and been inspired by pastors who come to retirement with joy in their hearts, gratitude on their lips, and a lilt in their step. I am grateful to be one of them. I look back on forty-three years of pastoral ministry as a long and joyful obedience. I can sing with the psalmist, "The boundary lines have fallen for me in pleasant places" (Ps. 16:6, NRSV). Even in times when the places haven't been entirely "pleasant," God has always managed to turn them into something good. In my seventh decade of life I'm singing an old gospel song titled "I Wouldn't Take Nothin' for My Journey Now."

So we must ask ourselves this: What spiritual and personal resources will keep us going over the long haul of ministry? How do we build spiritual disciplines and personal relationships that will continue to inspire us when the high, holy moments fade, and we find ourselves in the long days of ordinary time? What keeps us going when the going gets tough? How can we experience a life that is really worth living in the long obedience of ministry? We'll explore some of the answers to these questions in the weeks ahead.

Questions for Journaling

- Where and when did you begin to follow Christ?
- When have you identified with Demas in your life and ministry?

• Name the persons you know who have thrived in the long obedience to ministry.

Prayer

O God, who called me to follow your Son, Jesus Christ, in the long obedience of discipleship, even as you grabbed hold of me, so I grab onto your ongoing purpose for my life. By the power of your Holy Spirit, give me the inner strength to follow wherever you lead, trusting that my tomorrows are known to you, through Christ my Lord. Amen.

Day 1: Stir Up the Fire Within

Read 2 Timothy 1:1-14.

Perhaps Timothy was going through a fallow season. Perhaps the ordinary days of ministry had worn away the warm-hearted glow with which Paul's protégé began. Perhaps the opposition had become too intense. What we know is that Paul writes a letter to rekindle the fire in Timothy's heart and to reenergize his ministry. He begins by reminding Timothy of the faith he received from his mother and grandmother. A country proverb says that when we find a turtle sitting on a fence post, we know it didn't get there by itself. No one begins a life of faith or a calling to ministry *ex nihilo,* out of nothing. Faith begins as a gift we receive, not as a goal we achieve.

I'm a Timothy kind of disciple. I grew up attending a Methodist camp meeting where I responded to countless altar calls in search of a spiritual transformation like Paul's experience on the Damascus Road (see Acts 9:1-9). I rejoice with people who experience Christ that way. But there's no evidence Timothy had a blinding-light experience. Instead, Paul tells him to stir up the gift he received from his mother and grandmother.

I'm humbled by the memory of people who ignited the flame of faith in me: parents who loved me into the faith and supported God's call in my life; Sunday school teachers, camp counselors, professors, and preachers who challenged me to think, learn, and grow; friends who have walked with me; saints in the congregations I served who encouraged my gifts and cantankerous folks who forced me to see things I didn't want to see. With Paul, "I was made a minister according to the gift of God's grace which was given me" (Eph. 3:7, RSV).

In Methodist traditions, the call begins in the individual but is confirmed by others through the structures of the church. When the bishop lays hands on our head in the ritual of ordination, it means the call we felt in our soul has been affirmed and nurtured by faithful people along the way. Sometimes we kept going because we knew we didn't get into this on our own. Faithful sisters and brothers can remind us that we weren't wrong when we heard God's call.

The most painful transition of my life came when I had to move from the congregation I had helped birth. It meant leaving behind the community in which my wife and I raised our children and built lifelong friendships. The trust in myself that I had gained in leading that congregation over the years evaporated when we pulled out of the driveway. The road ahead looked uncertain and difficult. At the moment I needed it the most, a pastor friend introduced me to the song "For the Sake of the Call" by Steven Curtis Chapman.

I listened to that song over and over again as a renewing reminder of God's call in my life. It reignited my desire to follow wherever God might lead. It was a means of grace by which the Holy Spirit rekindled the fiery promise that "God did not give us a spirit of cowardice, but rather a spirit of power and of love and of self-discipline" (2 Tim. 1:7, NRSV).

Questions for Journaling

- Listen to a recording of "For the Sake of the Call" and allow the words to lead you into a time of prayer.
- Who were the people who passed the faith on to you and encouraged your call to ministry?
- How have you experienced the "rekindling" of God's gifts in your life and ministry?

Prayer

O Thou who camest from above,
the pure celestial fire to impart,
kindle a flame of sacred love
upon the mean altar of my heart.
Jesus, confirm my heart's desire
to work, and speak, and think for thee;
still let me guard the holy fire,
and still stir up thy gift in me.

—Charles Wesley (UMH, no. 501)

Day 2 : Busy with What?

Read Luke 10:38-42.

Martha is busy in the kitchen fixing supper for Jesus and his disciples while Mary sits in the living room listening to Jesus teach. I picture Martha dusting the flour off her apron and using the back of her hand to wipe the perspiration from her forehead as she steps through the doorway and grumbles, "Lord, don't you care that I'm doing all the work around here? How about telling my sister to get busy and help in the kitchen!" (Luke 10:40, AP). I doubt Martha appreciates Jesus' response: "Martha, Martha, you are worried and distracted by many things. One thing is necessary. Mary has chosen the better part. It won't be taken away from her" (Luke 10:41).

The location of this story is not a coincidence. Luke places it immediately after the parable of the good Samaritan with its concluding command, "Go and do likewise" (Luke 10:37). It is followed by Jesus' response to the request, "Lord, teach us to pray" (Luke 11:1). These three back-to-back stories portray the essential rhythm of being and doing, of prayer and action, of listening to Jesus' words and doing what Jesus says to do. It is the rhythm that sustains us over the long obedience of ministry.

This rhythm is difficult for hyperactive, get-the-job-done disciples to maintain. When we become preoccupied with all the good things we need to accomplish, we neglect our need for meditation on scripture and contemplative prayer. We tend to be "go-and-do-thou-likewise" people who measure effectiveness by how busy we become. The symbols in the needlepoint kneeling cushions at one church I served include a beehive with tiny bees buzzing around it. The woman who designed the cushions told me she wanted to remind people who came for prayer that they should be as busy as bees in the work of the kingdom.

I hear Jesus' words to Martha not as a rebuke but as an invitation to find the energy to do the work to which he calls us by being present with him through scripture and prayer. T. S. Eliot pointed to our need for quiet spaces when he asked,

> Where shall the word be found, where will the word
> Resound? Not here, there is not enough silence.[3]

Eugene H. Peterson affirmed the link between prayer and action when he wrote, "A contemplative life is not an alternative to the active life, but its root and foundation. . . . The contemplative life generates and releases . . . the enlivening energy of God's grace rather than the enervating frenzy of our pride."[4]

Vida Dutton Scudder (1861–1954) is remembered in the Episcopal Church as a person who demonstrated the Martha-Mary rhythm of social activism and spiritual discipline. She was a professor at Wellesley College, a prolific writer, and a leader in the Social Gospel Movement. But with all of her activism, she also wrote, "If prayer is the deep secret creative force that Jesus tells us it is, we should be very busy with it."[5]

What if the only effective way to be busy doing Christ's work is to be just as busy with prayer?

Questions for Journaling

- How do Jesus' words to Martha make you feel?
- Who have you known who practiced the rhythm of prayer and action?
- What can you stop doing so that you can be busy with prayer?

Prayer

We pray, O God, that Thou wilt fill this sacred minute with meaning, and make it an oasis for the refreshment of our souls, a window

cleaning for our vision, and a recharging of the batteries of our spir-
its. Let us have less talking and more thinking, less work and more
worship, less pressure and more prayer. For if we are too busy to
pray, we are far busier than we have any right to be. . . . Amen.

—Peter Marshall (1902–1949)[6]

Day 3: Dancing with the Trinity[7]

Read John 14:1-21; 16:5-16.

Most Christians I know do not need more encouragement to pray. They need more help in developing their own way of praying. I've found guidance in Jesus' description of the life-giving interaction of the Father, Son, and Holy Spirit.

Gregory of Nazianzus (329–390) used the word *perichoresis* to describe the relationship of the three persons of the Trinity. The Greek root words mean "to go around." Over the years, the word has acquired another interpretation: *dance*. In my book *A Disciple's Heart: Growing in Love and Grace, Companion Reader*, I compare Gregory's image of the Trinity to the sculpture *Three Dancing Maidens* in the Untermyer Fountain found in New York City's Central Park.[8] The statues inspire me to see prayer as a way of joining the dance of the Father, Son, and Holy Spirit. Practicing prayer is similar to the way dancers learn basic steps and then, as they grow more closely in tune with each other and the music, their dancing takes on its own unique style and flows with beauty, freedom, and joy.

Praying as a way of dancing with the Trinity begins with God the Creator (Father). My attention lifts beyond myself and centers in the goodness and greatness of the Almighty God. Beginning by praying the Psalms breaks my preoccupation with myself and lifts my attention toward God. I generally repeat the lectionary psalm for the week every day. The psalmist's words open my spirit to the presence of God.

Praying with God the Son centers my prayer in Jesus, God in human flesh. Meditating on scripture shapes my praying in ways that are consistent with the words, will, and way of the one who shows us the way of prayer (see Matthew 6:1-14; Luke 11:1-13; Luke 22:39-46). We pray as Jesus prayed so that we might live as Jesus lived. Listening to what Jesus says empowers us to do what Jesus would do.

Praying with God the Holy Spirit creates space in my life for the Holy Spirit to do what Jesus promises (see John 16:5-16). The Spirit draws me into God's ongoing work of compassion, justice, healing, and hope for our world. The power of the Holy Spirit connects me with the needs of others and empowers me to be an agent of God's love in the world (see Romans 8:18-27). Dancing with the Trinity through prayer breaks my bondage to self-interest and opens me to the way God is at work in the world.

Peter Storey, who led the Methodists of South Africa during the struggle against apartheid, wrote that his wife, Elizabeth, "understood that prayer for others is more than tossing some names at God. Real prayer is to carry somebody's need intimately, patiently and painfully in one's heart, holding them in love and lifting them tenderly and consistently into the light of God's grace. Real prayer costs and Elizabeth was willing to pay its price."[9]

Questions for Journaling

- How does the metaphor of dancing with the Trinity change your understanding of prayer?
- How do the words, way, and life of Jesus shape your experience of the Trinity?
- What practical steps will you take to choreograph your dance of prayer?

Prayer

Maker, in whom we live, in whom we are and move,
   the glory, power, and praise receive for thy creating love. . . .

Incarnate Deity, let all the ransomed race
    render in thanks their lives to thee for thy redeeming
    grace. . . .
Spirit of Holiness, let all thy saints adore
    thy sacred energy, and bless thine heart-renewing power.
                                    —Charles Wesley (UMH, no. 88)

Day 4: A Conspiracy of Love

Read Ecclesiastes 4:12; John 15:9-17.

Here's the bad news: We can't make it through the long obedience of ministry alone. Here's the good news: We don't have to! In fact, God never intended for us to make it on our own.

When E. Stanley Jones listed the experiences that shaped his life as a follower of Christ and sustained him across the years of his global witness, he pointed to the power of small-group fellowship modeled after John Wesley's class meetings. Jones defined these groups as "a fellowship in which people are 'unreservedly committed to Christ and unbreakably committed to each other.'"[10] Jones underscored the necessity of this kind of community when he wrote, "Everyone needs a group fellowship in which the group is in a conspiracy of love to make and keep each member the best person he is capable of being. If anyone hasn't such a group fellowship, he should find or create one; life demands it."[11]

The writer of the Old Testament book of Ecclesiastes provided the visual image of the strength we find in being bound together with a few other people as a "three-ply cord" that doesn't snap easily. Sadly, I've known too many people for whom the cord snapped along the way. Their calling was clear; their gifts were abundant; their passion for ministry was strong; their work was effective. But the cord snapped. They crashed on the hard rocks of personal moral failure, or they simply wore out beneath "the strain of toil, the fret of care" (UMH, no. 430). Some of them came to the end of their ministry under a dark cloud of disappointment, resentment, or bitterness, simply holding on until they had put in enough years to earn their pension.

Some of these people tried to do it alone. They did not have a circle of friends with whom they could share their joy and pain, success and failure, hopes and fears. Some of them seemed to live in a pious bubble that never allowed space for authentic friendships with people in their congregations. Some of them fell for temptation or made stupid mistakes that could have been prevented if they had allowed wiser, more experienced colleagues or friends to provide a sounding board when making decisions. They needed a "conspiracy of love" that enables each person to become the best person she or he is capable of becoming.

Members of the clergy covenant group in which I've participated for more than three decades remember the time one of our brothers began to describe a course of action he was considering that could have led to disaster. Another brother shouted across the room, "Are you out of your mind?" That outburst of loving honesty saved the other pastor for future ministry.

The power to make it over the long haul joyfully is a gift we give to each other in a conspiracy of love.

Questions for Journaling

- When have you experienced the strength, encouragement, or accountability of Christian friendship?
- Name a person who has provided strength for you and a person for whom you have been a strengthening friend.
- Pray for the Holy Spirit to guide you to find people with whom you can share a "conspiracy of love."

Prayer

Help us to help each other, Lord,
each other's cross to bear;
let all their friendly aid afford,
and feel each other's care.

Touched by the lodestone of thy love,
let all our hearts agree,
and ever toward each other move,
and ever move toward thee.

—Charles Wesley (UMH, no. 561)

Day 5: O Begin!

Read Matthew 6:5-6.

John Trembath failed as a Methodist preacher, but John Wesley never gave up on him as a follower of Christ. When Trembath joined the Methodist movement in 1743, he was a powerful preacher with a persuasive personal presence. But in 1755, Wesley wrote a stern letter in which he reminded Trembath of a time when he was "simple of heart and willing to spend and be spent for Christ," but he had been damaged by his "natural vanity" and "constitutional stubbornness."[12] Wesley diagnosed Trembath's problem as a lack of reading and daily prayer. He challenged Trembath to "recover the life of God in your own soul, and walk as Christ walked."[13] Later in the letter, Wesley's exclamation points convey the urgency in his words: "O choose the better part!—now!—to-day!"[14]

Five years later, Wesley wrote again, "You cannot stand still. . . . You must go forward or backward. Either you must recover that power, and be a Christian altogether; or in a while you will have neither power nor form, inside nor outside."[15] Wesley's challenge to Trembath is as true today as it was 250 years ago.

> O begin! Fix some part of every day for private exercises. . . . What is tedious at first, will afterwards be pleasant. Whether you like it or no, read and pray daily. It is for your life; there is no other way; else you will be a trifler all your days. . . . Do justice to your own soul; give it time and means to grow. Do not starve yourself any longer. Take up

your cross, and be a Christian altogether. Then will all the children of God rejoice (not grieve) over you.[16]

Michelle Shrader affirmed the importance of Wesley's daily discipline of reading and prayer during the three years she served on the staff of Central Methodist Mission in the heart of Cape Town, South Africa, as a short-term missionary with the United Methodist Board of Global Ministries. While actively engaged in the issues of social and economic injustice that continue to be the evil grandchildren of apartheid, she described her morning ritual that sustained her over the long haul.

I arise early in the morning with my cup of coffee to spend time in quiet and in devotional reading. I am regular in prayer for the needs of those in my life and the needs of our world around us. I read the paper or watch the morning news as a part of my disciplined way of life because I believe we must know what is happening in our world in order that we might be able to lead in it. I fast from the news if I find I am losing my center for engaging too much in information overload. Quiet was a discipline that I acquired over time and with practice.

Wherever we find ourselves along the journey of ministry, now is the time to begin or begin again the disciplines of reading scripture and prayer. As Mr. Wesley said, "It is for your life; there is no other way."

Questions for Journaling

- How do Wesley's words to Trembath speak to your life?
- What steps will you take to develop your own pattern of daily scripture reading and prayer?
- Who will you invite to hold you accountable to the decisions you make?

Prayer

O God, whose power and presence fills the whole creation, I need this quiet time with you to bring order to the chaos of my life, to calm my anxious spirit, to guide my restless mind, and to strengthen me for the tasks to which you have called me. I open myself to your presence that I might be filled with your power, through Jesus Christ my Lord. Amen.

Week 2   People

I was living in a world redolent with spirituality. There
were no ordinary people.

—Eugene H. Peterson

Relationships in the Spirit of the Trinity

Read Psalm 138; John 13:31-35, 14:1-31.

In a classic *Peanuts* comic strip, Linus tells Lucy, "I love mankind. It's people I can't stand!!"[1]

We may feel called to ministry because we experience an expansive, all-inclusive, extraordinary love for humanity. But soon enough we find ourselves in ordinary time, serving an ordinary congregation where love for humanity takes form in ordinary relationships with ordinary people. The church turns out to be a bizarre and often frustrating menagerie of saints and sinners, joy bringers and joy drainers, people who lift others up and people who wear others down, pilgrims processing powerfully into the future and protectionists pointing persistently to the past. Some are loving, joyful, and generous; some are mean, manipulative, and downright crazy!

That's when we wrestle with the fact that ministry is persistently personal and relentlessly relational. Whatever else we are called to do, our primary task is to incarnate God's perfect love in relationships with imperfect people. Holiness takes shape with unholy people who are on the way toward holiness, and we are among them.

James Weldon Johnson captured the relational character of God in his poem "The Creation." He heard God say, "I'm lonely— I'll make me a world."[2] God delights in all facets of the Creation, then realizes that loneliness remains. God's remedy was to create human beings. The Bible begins with a lonely God for whom the whole of blooming creation is incomplete without people to share it. Jesus describes the relational nature of God the Father, Son, and Holy Spirit during the Last Supper with his most intimate human companions (see John 15:26–16:16). I'm convinced that the Trinity is not just a theological construct to define the nature of God but an image that reveals how God intends for us to be in relationship with one another. So, what would it mean to see our relationships in the likeness of the Trinity?

First, the Trinity is mysterious. It's always beyond our explanation, though never beyond our experience. There is always more to see than we have seen, always more to know than we already know. An eighteenth-century German hymn based on the fourth-century Latin *Te Deum Laudamus* calls us to unashamedly "own the mystery."

> Holy Father, Holy Son, Holy Spirit:
> three we name thee,
> though in essence only one;
> undivided God we claim thee,
> and adoring bend the knee
> while we own the mystery. (UMH, no. 79)

People are mysterious too. Henri J. M. Nouwen observed, "The mystery of one [person] is too immense and too profound to be explained by another [person]."[3] Across the years I've attempted to "own the mystery" of people—who they are, where they came from, how they have been hurt or healed, and where they are going in their faith. I try to enter relationships with more curiosity than analysis in order to discover more than what is initially seen and to know people beyond the limits of what is immediately known. I'm often surprised (and sometimes disappointed) in what I find, but it makes a difference in me to live with a sense of mystery not unlike the way I "own the mystery" of the Trinity.

Second, seeing human relationships in the likeness of the Trinity calls for humility, a beautiful virtue that is sadly in short supply today. There is a time and place for intellectual attempts to explain the Trinity, but we experience the Trinity best when we sing, "Holy, holy, holy! Lord God Almighty" or when we are humbled by God's greatness the way Isaiah experiences God in the Temple (see Isaiah 6:1-7).

Paul expresses genuine humility not phony piety when he acknowledges, "I'm the least important of the apostles. . . . I am what I am by God's grace" (1 Cor. 15:9-10). That kind of humility grows from knowing who God is and who he is so that by God's grace he can overcome the arrogant self-assurance masking his insecurity and blocking healthy relationships with others. Humility is not pretending to think less of ourselves but thinking more of others. Relating to people with reverent humility means that we value them as one-of-a-kind creations whose ordinary human lives contain something of the extraordinary image of God—even the people who are most difficult. Reverent humility enables us to listen.

When I arrived at my first pastoral appointment as an excited, inexperienced, insecure seminary graduate attempting to prove that I knew more than I did, I met Ernest Cadman Colwell (1901–1974). A leading authority on the Greek New Testament, he taught in the School of Theology and served as president at the University of Chicago, and he was the founding President of Claremont School of Theology. He could not have been more welcoming or less condescending to a green-as-grass associate pastor. But did I latch onto him as a wealth of knowledge and experience to help shape my future ministry? I'm disappointed to confess that because of my insecurity and immature efforts to prove my own competence, I missed out on what could have been a formative relationship if I had demonstrated a little more humility.

Third, the Trinity calls us to relationships animated by love. Jesus' teaching about the Trinity comes in the context of his new commandment: "Love each other. Just as I have loved you, so you also must love each other. This is how everyone will know that you are my disciples, when you love each other" (John 13:34-35). The epistle of John calls us to relationships that model the character of the God who is love (see 1 John 4:8). Paul writes the words of First

Corinthians 13 not for wedding ceremonies but to describe relationships in the body of Christ. All these scripture passages point to the love for which Charles Wesley prayed,

> To love is all my wish,
> I only live for this . . .
>
> Thy power I pant to prove
> Rooted and fixed in love . . .
>
> Ah! Give me this to know
> With all they saints below.
> Swells my soul to compass thee,
>   Gasps in thee to live and move,
> Filled with all the deity,
>   All immersed and lost in love![4]

While visiting an elder saint in a church I served, I said, "You've seen a lot of preachers come and go, haven't you?" She replied, "Oh, yes!" I continued, "And I'll bet you loved every one of them." She paused before she responded with a sly smile, "Some of them were easier to love than others!" Her words are true for both pastors and church members. Some were "love at first sight." They loved me before I gave them any reason to love me. Others were people I learned to love as we shared life together. And then there were some I never really learned to love. The best I could do was practice kindness or patience with them. I also know that's how people related with me. In the complexities of human relationships, our goal is for the perfect love of God to be at work in our imperfect human relationships.

Faith in the Trinity calls us to relate to people with mystery, humility, and love. What a beautiful way to live!

Questions for Journaling

- How was love for people a part of your calling to ministry?
- How does your experience of the Trinity shape your relationships with people?

• How have you experienced mystery, humility, and love in relationships with the people you serve?

Prayer

Grant us humility, knowing that we have not yet attained; shame us from our pride by a fresh vision of our possibilities; and since what we are is but the seed of what we may grow to be, grant us the inspiration of his Spirit, who gives to them that receive him power to become the [children] of God. Amen.

—Harry Emerson Fosdick (1878–1969)[5]

Day 1: The Dragnet of Grace

Read Matthew 4:18-25; 2 Corinthians 5:14-17.

"People who need people are the luckiest people in the world," goes the song "People," first made popular by Barbra Streisand.[6] Fill in the blank in this sentence: Pastors who need people are the _____ people in the world. Sometimes the adjective could be *richest* or *happiest*. I am immeasurably grateful for the amazing people I never would have met if I had not been their pastor. Sometimes the adjective could be *loneliest* or *most frustrated*. A pastoral mentor taught me this saying:

> To be there above with the people we love,
>   That will be glory!
> To be here below with the people we know,
>   That's another story!

The burden and blessing of pastoral ministry are that it always includes ordinary people. Jesus calls his disciples to leave the fishing-for-fish business and get into the fishing-for-people business. At one point, they decide to go back to catching fish, which at least suggests that we'll have some of those days too! But the risen Christ restores the disciples to their calling and sends them out again to become the best people-fishers of all time (see John 21:1-19).

I've sometimes wished I could be a pastoral fly fisherman, catching carefully selected people and reeling them in one at a time. But Jesus says the kingdom of God is like the nets I've seen dragged across the floor of the Gulf of Mexico gathering up "all kinds of fish"

(Matt. 13:47). A church in which everyone likes me or is like me leaves too many people outside the dragnet of grace. It would also be incredibly boring. I prefer the creativity, confusion, and chaos of a dragnet church that gathers up all kinds of people. The congregation in Corinth is a dragnet full of all kinds of people with all kinds of issues. But Paul declares that because "the love of Christ controls us" and because we know Christ "died for the sake of all," we no longer see people "by human standards" (2 Cor. 5:14, 16). We drag the net of God's universal love and grace through the world, gathering up all kinds along the way, seeing in their ordinary lives the possibility of the extraordinary life of new creation.

Art historians say that when Leonardo da Vinci was painting *The Last Supper* on the refectory wall in the convent of Santa Maria delle Grazie in Milan, he found the faces of the disciples in the streets of the city. Looking carefully at all kinds of people, da Vinci could see something no one else could see. He saw the faces of disciples. Among them he even found the face of Jesus. What a difference it makes if we can see the face of a disciple in the faces of all the people who end up in the dragnet of grace.

Questions for Journaling

- Like the disciples, when have you found yourself questioning your calling? How has Jesus restored you to your calling?
- How does the metaphor of fishing for people speak to you?
- Write down the names of people who bring you joy and are easy to love. Make another list of the names of people who are difficult for you to love. Spend time lifting each name in prayer, and record in your journal the way the Spirit of God either is or could be active in those relationships.

Prayer

O God, whose love became flesh in Jesus, by the power of your Holy Spirit enable me to see the face of Christ in the faces of people around me. Amen.

Day 2: The Many and the Few

Read Mark 3:7-19.

Mark paints two contrasting portraits of Jesus. In one we see Jesus amid a massive crowd of all kinds of people from all kinds of places with all kinds of needs. In the contrasting portrait, Jesus is on an isolated hillside where he calls the twelve disciples. Out of the many, Jesus chooses a few so that through them his power will be released among the many. For the sake of the many, Jesus pours himself into the few.

Thriving in the long obedience of ministry depends on the alternating rhythm of life shared with all kinds of people in all kinds of relationships and life shared in the intimacy of particular people with whom we share God's mission. This rhythm became a reality for me through surprising advice I received at two critical moments in my ministry.

When I was working on birthing a new church, an experienced pastor warned me that the spiritual and human DNA that are planted in the early roots of a congregation will continue to shape its life long into the future. He said bluntly, "Don't let the 'crazies' take control!" A new congregation can be a magnet for unhealthy or toxic people who come with personal agendas. My responsibility was to enable spiritually healthy people to form the leadership core of the church so that it could become a place where unhealthy folks would find healing. It meant focusing attention on people who love God and love others more than they love themselves; people who are growing in spiritual disciplines; people who demonstrate a generosity of spirit and a desire to serve others; people who catch a vision of God's mission for that church. They also need to be joyful people with a sense of humor who don't take themselves too seriously. We equip leaders not on the basis of our personal preferences but on the basis of their spiritual and emotional health and their commitment to God's mission.

The second word of advice came when I was appointed to a ninety-three-year-old congregation that needed to reclaim its mission and vision. A wise mentor told me that in leading through change, we don't need a majority; we need "critical mass." *The New York Times* columnist David Brooks described "critical mass" when he wrote, "Culture changes when a small group of people . . . find a better way to live, and other people begin to copy them."[7] Build critical mass and, like Jesus' parable of the yeast in the loaf, it will begin to impact the whole. Instead of attempting to change people who didn't want to be changed or to win unanimous approval for everything, I focused my energy on faithful people who could inspire a new vision within the rest of the congregation. Those leaders became the circle of accountability for my leadership.

My circle of accountability included long-time, spiritually mature, highly respected members of the church who were passionately committed to its future. They loved me enough to encourage me in difficult times and to correct me when I got it wrong. I knew that if I was in sync with them, I was heading in the right direction. They were the few who helped welcome the many into the body of Christ.

Questions for Journaling

• How are you balancing ministry with the many and the few?
• How have you seen the importance of what is implanted in the DNA of a congregation?
• Who are the few people who can help you capture God's vision for the church and hold you accountable in love?

Prayer

Living Lord, who called the few to extend your love and healing to the many, bring into my life the critical mass of healthy disciples who will hold me accountable to your vision and be the agents of your grace in the lives of others. Amen.

Day 3: The People and the Mission

Read John 13:1; 15:9-17; 16:31-33.

One of the best gifts of pastoral ministry in my life has been the diverse people I've loved and who have loved me along the way. Bill Studer was one of them. Every time we met, he would grab my hand, pull me close, break out his day-brightening smile, and say, "I love you, man!" This outburst wasn't what I expected from a retired Major General who across thirty-three years in the Air Force had accumulated five thousand hours in the air as a command pilot, more than one thousand of those in Vietnam. As commander of Clark Air Base in the Philippines, he was responsible for the evacuation of twenty-five thousand civilians and military personnel when Mount Pinatubo erupted in 1991. Having received just about every award the military can give, he retired as director of operations at United States Central Command in Tampa, became an active member of my congregation, and claimed me as his pastor and friend. Even if we disagreed about a particular political issue, we'd never see each other when he wouldn't tell me again that he loved me.

One of the first things I learned about Bill was his unshakable love for the men and women under his command. He called them his "kids." He cared passionately about them and was determined to use every ounce of his energy, influence, and experience to support them, particularly when they went into battle.

Bill faced his death with the same ruthless honesty and joyful courage with which he had lived the rest of his life. In our last visit before his death, I asked if he had any idea how many people he had led across his career. All he could say was, "Thousands!" When I asked what he had learned through that experience, he immediately said, "Take care of the people, and the people will take care of the mission." He said some leaders put the mission first and use people to accomplish it, but he had learned that once the mission is clear, his job was to support the people and give them what they needed in order to accomplish it.

That didn't mean that Bill didn't have high expectations and hold people accountable. He said, "I never hesitated to fire people who weren't in the right place. It wasn't personal. They just weren't right for the job." Though he couldn't fire me, he never hesitated to let me know when he thought I was missing the mark, but I never doubted that he loved me just the way he loved the people he led.

Remembering Bill's friendship, I'm drawn to the way Jesus loves his disciples, even when he knows they are heading into harm's way. They are not servants to be commanded, manipulated, or used but friends with whom he shares a common mission. Looking directly into the face of the suffering that both he and his disciples will confront, Jesus openly expresses his unshakable love for them. I can imagine his face breaking out in a day-brightening smile when he says, "Be of good cheer; I have overcome the world" (John 16:33, KJV).

Questions for Journaling

- What emotions do you feel when you read Jesus' last words to his disciples?
- How have you experienced leaders who put people first?
- What will it mean for you to lead people the way Jesus did?

Prayer

O God, teach me to be a leader like Jesus, a leader who loves others with an unshakable love and equips them to serve others with unrelenting strength and joy. Amen.

Day 4: You've Got a Friend

Read Proverbs 18:24; 1 Samuel 18:1-3.

To make it through the long and joyful obedience of ministry we really need friends. Singer-songwriter James Taylor received an amazing gift from a friend when Carole King gave him a song he's been singing ever since: "You've Got a Friend." She said, "The song was as close to pure inspiration as I've ever experienced. The song wrote itself. It was written by something outside myself, through me."[8] I think that's what we mean when we say something is inspired by the Holy Spirit.

I doubt that either King or Taylor had heard of Aelred, the twelfth-century saint who gave the Middle Ages its classic description of friendship. Born in 1109, he was educated in the upper-class life of the court, but he became disillusioned with royal life and experienced a dark night of soul-searching. He emerged to become a Cistercian monk in 1133 and soon became a spiritual and ecclesiastical leader in the English church. His book *Spiritual Friendship* became a spiritual classic that continues to be in print today.

Aelred described spiritual friendship as a combination of God's gift and human effort. While God's love is universally available to everyone, he saw Christian friendship as a unique love shared among individuals with deep intimacy and spiritual discipline. He compared it to the relationship between Jesus and John at the Last Supper. I also see it in the Old Testament friendship between David and Jonathan.

Aelred named four essential characteristics of spiritual friendship: loyalty, right intention, discretion, and patience. To Aelred's characteristics I would add joy. As a person who inherited a genetic sense of Germanic seriousness, I need friends who bring laughter and joy into my life. I've decided that life is too short to be friends with people who don't make me smile when they come through the door.

When I am asked to name the factors that have shaped and sustained me across the long haul of ministry, Christian friendship is right at the top of the list. I would place it among the sacraments, which is where Jesus places it during the Last Supper when he tells the disciples, "I don't call you servants any longer. . . . Instead, I call you friends" (John 15:15).

When we find a person who practices loyalty, right intention, discretion, and patience and who brings us joy, we know we've got a friend.

Questions for Journaling

- What difference does it make for you to think of friendship as a sacrament?
- How would you rewrite Aelred's characteristics of friendship in your own words?
- Who brings joy into your life?

Prayer for St. Aelred's Day

Almighty God, you endowed the abbot Aelred with the gift of Christian friendship and the wisdom to lead others in the way of holiness: Grant to your people that same spirit of mutual affection, that, in loving one another, we may know the love of Christ and rejoice in the gift of your eternal goodness; through the same Jesus Christ our Savior, who lives and reigns with you and the Holy Spirit, one God, now and for ever. Amen.[9]

Day 5: Sometimes You Need to Be Alone

Read Mark 6:29-32.

I take it as good news that sometimes Jesus has to get away from people.

The "breaking news" of the murder of John the Baptist reaches Jesus and the disciples during some of the busiest days of their ministry. So many people are coming and going that they don't have time to eat. We all have days like that. But Matthew records that when Jesus gets the news that John has been beheaded, "he withdrew in a boat to a deserted place by himself" (14:13). He has to deal with the word of his cousin's gruesome death alone. In Mark's version, Jesus invites the disciples, saying, "Come by yourselves to a secluded place and rest for a while" (6:31). Leaving the crowds behind, "they departed in a boat by themselves for a deserted place" (Mark 6:32).

Tracking the times Jesus spends time by himself or with only his most intimate followers would make an interesting Bible study. In these moments of solitude, Jesus wrestles with major decisions, seeks renewal through silence in the presence of God, prepares for the cross, or simply pursues a break from the crowds. If Jesus needs time alone to rest, refresh, and renew his soul, what makes us think we don't need it too?

Inspired by the song "Let Me Burn Out for Thee," I came into ministry believing that it was better to burn out than to rust out.

I'm grateful for the urgency that was planted in my heart, a burning passion for people to know and follow Christ and for my life to make a kingdom-shaped difference in the world. That urgency has been a source of strength during the ordinary times when it seemed that very little I was doing made much difference. I'd still rather burn out than rust out.

But I've also learned that ministry is a marathon, not a twenty-yard dash. After working myself into a midlife depression and a physical collapse, I had to accept the fact that my body is not an inexhaustible machine. My wife reminded me that I was married before I was ordained and that being a husband, father, and grandfather is God's first call in my life. I've found that in a hyperactive, overachieving culture, the witness of a more peaceful, well-balanced life is the most desperately needed witness I can give.

When we feel as if we have to be serving others all the time, we can listen for Jesus calling us to come away to a quiet place and rest. If it was good enough for Jesus, it's good enough for us.

Questions for Journaling

- What urgency energizes your ministry?
- How does Jesus' need for solitude impact your understanding of him?
- What do you do to sustain your soul? What steps to you need to take to create quiet space in your life?

Prayer

O sabbath rest by Galilee,
O calm of hills above,
where Jesus knelt to share with thee
the silence of eternity,
interpreted by love!

Drop thy still dews of quietness,
till all our strivings cease;
take from our souls the strain and stress,

and let our ordered lives confess
the beauty of thy peace.

Breathe through the heats of our desire
thy coolness and thy balm;
let sense be dumb, let flesh retire;
speak through the earthquake, wind, and fire,
O still, small voice of calm.

—John Greenleaf Whittier (UMH, no. 358)

Week 3   Place

All theology is rooted in geography. . . . Your place is that without which you could not do your work.

—Eugene H. Peterson

Where I'm From

Read Genesis 28:16-17.

Have you noticed the way our biblical forebears named places? Right at the beginning in the book of Genesis, we see characters giving extraordinary names to ordinary places that become holy places because they are places where people encounter the presence of God.

- "That place was called Beer-sheba; because there [Abraham and Abimelech] swore an oath" (Gen. 21:31, NRSV).
- "Abraham called that place 'The Lord will provide'; as it is said to this day, 'On the mount of the Lord it shall be provided'" (Gen. 22:14, NRSV).
- "Jacob woke from his sleep and said, 'Surely the Lord is in this place—and I did not know it!' And he was afraid, and said, 'How awesome is this place! This is none other than the house of God, and this is the gate of heaven'" (Gen. 28:16-17, NRSV).
- "Jacob called the place Peniel, saying, 'For I have seen God face to face, and yet my life is preserved'" (Gen. 32:30, NRSV).
- "[Jacob] built an altar and called the place El-bethel, because it was there that God had revealed himself to him when he fled from his brother" (Gen. 35:7, NRSV).

Throughout the Old Testament, ordinary places became holy places where people found God or, more correctly, where God found them; places where they found themselves, made covenant relationships with others, and discovered what God was calling them to do; places where they found strength and hope for the long obedience of their faith.

In the New Testament, we cannot not tell the gospel story without naming ordinary, often out-of-the-way places where God's love became flesh among us: Bethlehem, the Sea of Galilee, a mountainside, an upper room, Gethsemane, Calvary, an empty tomb. We can't know who we are as the church without waiting in Jerusalem for Pentecost, standing with Peter on a rooftop in Joppa, listening to Paul in Athens and tracking his missionary travels around the Mediterranean Sea. We would not be sustained for the long journey of faith without going to the island of Patmos and catching a glimpse of John's vision of the new Jerusalem coming down from heaven.

Places matter. They locate infinity in finite time and space. They incarnate the divine in the mundane. During the Civil Rights movement Martin Luther King Jr. would hold a prayer service in the smoldering ruins of burned-down churches. People who attended those services might not remember exactly what Dr. King said, but they never forgot where he said it.[1] The place proclaimed the way God was present in a bruised and broken world.

I gained a new understanding of the works of Salvador Dali when the Dali Museum in St. Petersburg, Florida, hosted an exhibition of photographs of Dali's homeland by nature photographer Clyde Butcher, who is known as Florida's Ansel Adams. Butcher's black-and-white photographs revealed the way the landscape of Catalonia became an essential part of Dali's outlook on life and permeated his paintings. It reminded me of the way we are shaped and formed by the places our lives have taken us.

Holy places mark where we have been and point us in the direction we are called to go. We can each name them in our own journey. They are ordinary places that became extraordinary for us because, in Robert Frost's matchless words, "two roads diverged in a yellow wood" and we, for whatever reasons we thought we knew or could not fully comprehend at the time, chose one over the other, and that decision ended up making "all the difference."[2] In recounting the places his life took him, Timothy B. Tyson quotes Bernice

Johnson Reagon, who said, "If, in moving through your life, you find yourself lost, go back to the last place where you knew who you were, and what you were doing, and start from there."[3]

George Ella Lyon served as poet laureate of Kentucky from 2015 through 2017. Among her evocative poems is one titled "Where I'm From." In the summer of 1993, she was prompted by another poet to begin making lists of ordinary things, places, and names, phrases that marked the journey of her life. Over time she wove those lists into a poem that flows from the key phrase "I am from . . . ." She names ordinary things like "the Dutch elm . . . fried corn and strong coffee."[4] Lyon began inviting other people to make their own lists and from them to shape their personal version of the "Where I'm From" poem. People have used her pattern in classrooms, at family reunions, in prisons, and in refugee camps across the United States and around the world. The Kentucky Arts Council gathered 731 "Where I'm From" poems from eighty-three countries, forming uncommon ties through common things.

The first time I tried the "Where I'm From" exercise, the simplicity of it brought an unexpected lump in my throat and unanticipated tears to my eyes: tears of gratitude for gifts I had been given and tears of sadness for things I had forgotten and people or places I will never see again. Since then I've used it in retreats with church leaders, continuing education events for preachers, and Sunday school classes. I begin by asking someone, preferably a woman with a Southern drawl, to read Lyon's poem. Then I invite people to make lists of places that have been important to their faith journey, names of people who encouraged them along the way, words or phrases that stand out to them, or tastes and smells that linger in their memory. I give them time alone to write their own poem, starting with the words, "I am from . . . ."

In one group, a rough-hewn country preacher bluntly declared, "I don't do poetry." But because he was a part of the group, he said he'd give it a try. When the participants scattered across the campus to write their poems, I saw him concentrating on his lists, scratching his head, and then beginning to write. He was the last person to return to the group and one of the first to read his poem aloud. We were amazed by the way his words told the story of his life in his own unique way. When he finished, the entire group broke into applause. He found himself in describing where he was from.

Ministry happens in a particular place. We do not fulfill our calling in an esoteric world of spirituality that drifts in a cloud ten feet above the earth. The first and most persistent heresy refuted by the early Christians was Gnosticism, which promoted the idea that the real world is somewhere other than here; truth is quarantined in a mystical realm that never fully touches down to earth. By contrast, the radical word of the gospel is that when the infinite Word became flesh, it became finite, human flesh with human skin, hair, blood, and cells. The Word through which all creation came into being became a living, breathing, sweating, eating, and drinking human being in a particular time and place.

So it is for our ministries. They happen in real places where real human lives are connected to the life of Christ. God's call upon each of our lives is largely defined by where we are and where we're from. I've discovered one of the sources of strength for the long obedience of ministry is found in naming the places I've been, recalling the faces of people I've known, and reclaiming the ways ordinary places became holy places in my life.

Questions for Journaling

- Try the "Where I'm From" exercise for yourself. What did you discover?
- Where are the holy places in your life?
- How has your ministry been influenced by your past?

Prayer

When all thy mercies, O my God,
My rising soul surveys,
Transported with the view I'm lost
In wonder, love, and praise.

—Joseph Addison (1672–1719)[5]

Day 1: A Longing for Home

Read 1 Thessalonians 3:6-13;
Revelation 1:9-11; 21:1-7.

Geraldine Page won the 1986 Academy Award for Best Actress for her poignant portrayal of Mrs. Watts in the movie *The Trip to Bountiful*. It's the story of an elderly woman who wants, more than anything else, to make one last trip back to Bountiful, the long-gone Texas farm where she grew up. There was nothing overtly religious about the movie, except for the musical soundtrack that begins and ends the movie with an old gospel song:

Come home, come home;
you who are weary, come home;
earnestly, tenderly Jesus is calling,
calling, O sinner come home. (UMH, no. 348)

The story evokes the universal human desire to find our way to the place where we know who we are and that we are loved. Frederick Buechner called it "the longing for home." He said it's our life-long search for "the home we knew and will always long for" and "the home we dream of finding and for which we also long."[6]

For those of us who have ever been homesick, we can feel the emotion with which Paul writes to his friends in Thessalonica. "Do you have any idea how very homesick we became for you, dear friends? . . . You can't imagine how much we missed you!" (1 Thess. 2:17, MSG). So, Paul prays, "May God our Father himself and our Master Jesus clear the road to you!" (1 Thess. 3:11, MSG).

We see the same longing in the apostle John. He is a homesick political prisoner on the island of Patmos. Picture Nelson Mandela on Robben Island, Dietrich Bonhoeffer in a Nazi prison, or Martin Luther King Jr. in the Birmingham city jail. Like them and like Mrs. Watts, John longs for the home he remembers and the people he loves. At the same time, he is entranced by a vision of the home he dreams.

> "Look! God's dwelling is here with humankind. He will dwell with them, and they will be his peoples. God himself will be with them. . . . He will wipe away every tear from their eyes. Death will be no more. There will be no mourning, crying, or pain anymore, for the former things have passed away." (Rev. 21:3-4)

Throughout the long obedience of our faith, we carry within us the influence of the home we remember, the gifts of our past, and all the things that made us who we are. We can no more escape them than a turtle can escape its shell. At the same time, we live toward the future, always holding above and before us the hope of the home we dream; the promised day when God's kingdom comes and God's will is done on earth as it is in heaven and when God is fully at home among us.

The home we remember and the home we dream locate the places from which we have come and lure us to the places we are called to go. The invitation to each of us is "Come home."

Questions for Journaling

- When have you experienced a longing for home?
- How is your life shaped by "the home you remember"?
- How does "the home you dream" influence your ministry?

Prayer

O God, who is at home in every time and place, we carry with us the influence of the home we remember and give thanks for every way it has made us who we are. By the power of your Spirit, enable us to live in ways that bear witness to the home we dream, for the sake of Jesus Christ, the same yesterday, today, and forever. Amen.

Day 2: Living in the Land

Read Psalm 37:1-7, 37.

Places matter. We fulfill our calling in a particular place at a particular time with particular people. Eugene H. Peterson was primarily a pastor who challenged other pastors to "embrace the *locale*." He said that a pastor's work "is geographical as much as it is theological. . . . working things out in the particular soil of a particular parish. . . . this sense of place . . . immerses us in particulars and shapes our ministry."[7]

A sense of place should not surprise people who are rooted in scripture. God's self-revelation happens among real people, in real time, and in real places. In the same way, we are called to serve in real places among real people in real time. Some are places we choose; others are places to which we are sent.

I didn't choose Crescent City, Florida; I was sent there. The stoplight at the main intersection was the only stoplight along a sixty-mile stretch of Route 17. Former citrus groves were now ferneries, shipping decorative ferns to florists across the nation. The century-old congregation contained multigenerational families whose roots sank deep into the sandy soil of north central Florida. Two blocks from the red-brick church, the parsonage was a typical, one-story, white-frame Florida home under aged oak trees draped with Spanish moss and surrounded by azalea bushes that exploded with color in the spring. Built to catch the prevailing breezes before the advent of home air-conditioning, each room had large windows or doors that opened onto a screened porch.

Neither my wife nor I had ever lived in a place like this. At first, we felt oddly out of place. Did we really belong here? Could we connect with these people? Was this a place where we could joyfully invest the ordinary days of our lives? We had to choose. Would we spend our time wishing we were somewhere else? Or would we live fully into the community, learning all we could learn, enjoying everything there was to enjoy, and investing in relationships with the people who welcomed their young pastor and his family with open arms?

With the psalmist, we chose to "live in the land, and farm faithfulness" (Ps. 37:3). We decided not to pine for some other place or wish for something we didn't have but to be fully present in that place with those people. I visited in their homes, joined the Rotary Club, went fishing with old guys who knew the lake like the back of their hand, and looked forward to meeting our toddler daughters as I walked home for lunch along the sandy street between the church and the parsonage. I took advantage of the slow pace of life to develop patterns of daily scripture reading, prayer, study, and sermon preparation that continued throughout my ministry. And I found joy! I laughed, cried, and served with people whose friendships have endured across the years. It was the place where I became a pastor. The place my family and I were sent became a place for which we will always give thanks.

Questions for Journaling

- What things are most unique about the place you currently serve?
- Who are the people in this place who can help you grow?
- Where will you find joy?

Prayer

O God, who has planted me in this place, give me grace to live fully in it; to sink my roots deep into the soil of its life; to nurture the vine you planted here before I came; and to tend these branches with love and care, that by your Spirit I will be a blessing to it, and it will become a place of blessing for me. Amen.

Day 3: What Are We Doing Here?

Read John 15:1-8.

The most important question a ministry leader needs to ask is this: What are we doing here *today*? What is God calling us to do or to be in this place at this moment with these people? But we cannot answer that question in the present without digging into the past.

When I was appointed to birth a new congregation, I had the once-in-a-church's-lifetime opportunity to define its spiritual, theological, and missional DNA *de novo*, from the beginning. As that congregation enters its fourth decade, I can see how some of the trees I planted in the beginning have extended new branches as the church has grown and adapted to the rapidly changing community it serves.

Most of us don't have that opportunity. Most of us serve congregations that were in place long before we came on the scene. When I was appointed to a ninety-three-year-old congregation in a historically designated neighborhood of one of the oldest cities in Florida, I discovered the importance of congregational history. Just the way each of us has been shaped by the places we're from, the present life of a congregation grows out of its roots in the past. Discerning what God was calling us to do today needed to grow out of the longer story of what God had been doing there across the years. My task was to dig into the roots, to listen to the stories, to feel the beating of the congregation's heart, to search for the way the future would grow out of its past.

I found dead branches that needed to be trimmed; tragic stories of pain, conflict, and failure; stories to which the best response was, "Let the dead bury their own dead" (Matt. 8:22). Donna Claycomb Sokol found the same things when she arrived at Mount Vernon Place United Methodist Church in Washington, D.C. If the church were to have a future, there would need to be a lot of pruning. "The congregation needed to let go of . . . stuff crammed in closets and rooms, activities labeled as 'ministry,' several paid staff members. But no one could see the necessary changes yet but me."[8] Like Donna, I also discovered the stories that went to the taproot of the church's life, stories that had inspired the church when it was thriving and had sustained it when times were hard. From those stories, I was able to shape a fresh vision for the future that grew out of the best strengths of the past.

In my early years as a pastor, one of my mentors reminded me that the roots of the church had been established long before I got there and would hopefully continue to grow long after I was gone. He told me that I was called to tend the vine for this moment in time so that it could continue to bear fruit in the future. I quickly learned that tending the vine is not always easy, especially when the act of pruning becomes inevitable. It creates conflict with people who place a high value on the past. New branches grow slowly. They require relentless patience and constant attention. None of us is a perfect gardener; we make mistakes along the way. We have no guarantee that every branch on the vine will grow and bear fruit, but we do the best we can, trusting that God will use our tending of the vine to produce more fruit in the future. It's all we can do.

Questions for Journaling

- What stories from the past can help define your congregation's ministry in the future?
- Who are the people who can help you get in touch with the roots of your congregation?
- How will you tend the vine so that it can thrive in the future?

Prayer

O God, whose Spirit was at work in this place long before I arrived and will continue to be at work after I am gone, give me a grateful heart for all who have gone before me and give me an open mind to what you intend for the future. Don't let the past limit my vision but use what I have been to empower what you would have me become. I pray in the name of the risen Christ. Amen.

Day 4: A Table with a Window on the World

Read Isaiah 25:6-10; Revelation 7:9.

For all who experienced 9/11, the memory of the incalculable losses of that day has left an indelible scar on each of our souls. But as is often the case, the memory of a particular, comparatively insignificant loss can unlock the memories of the larger, all-encompassing loss of which it was a part. When some New Yorkers look up into the empty sky where the Twin Towers once stood, they hold a particular memory of their visits to the Windows on the World restaurant on the 106–107th floors of the North Tower. On a clear day, a table beside the floor-to-ceiling windows really felt like a table with a window on the whole world. In a similar way, the Table of our Lord can become the window through which we see the world.

Our place matters. It is the unique locale of our ministry, but it can also cramp our vision. The persistent risk in centering ourselves with particular people in a particular place is that we begin to think our place is the *only* place or that our place is the measure of all other places. Taking seriously the context where we serve can compress our attention to what is closest at hand, causing us to lose our connection to the larger world around us. It can reinforce sinful tendencies toward racism, nativism, and a sense of cultural superiority.

During seminary my wife and I spent a weekend with family friends who had recently returned from Vietnam where they served as missionaries. They were now serving a tiny, poverty-stricken coal-mining community in the hills of Eastern Kentucky. When we noticed copies of *National Geographic Magazine* on their coffee table, they said they wanted their children to grow up with visual reminders that they were part of a larger world. It was their table with a window on the world.

Isaiah experiences the vision of that kind of table as he dreams of a day when the Lord will host a spectacular banquet for "all peoples" (Isa. 25:6). On that day the Lord will remove the shroud of death from "all nations" (Isa. 25:7) and will wipe the tears from the eyes of "every face" (Isa. 25:8). John catches the same vision when he sees "a great crowd that no one could number . . . from every nation, tribe, people, and language" (Rev. 7:9).

While serving in a particular place, we need to remember that the biblical vision of heaven is more like the United Nations than any individual culture, race, or nation. If we don't like being among people of other races, colors, languages, nations, and cultures, heaven might not be the place for us. I'm convinced that hell is individual isolation in which our lives shrink down into the most miniscule remainder of our narrow self-interest. Wherever we serve, the Table of our Lord is a table with a window on the whole, wide, wonderful, wounded world. When we gather around that Table in our particular place, we are united with Jesus' followers in every place—people whose faces we will never see and whose names we will never know but brothers and sisters with whom we are "one in ministry to all the world, until Christ comes in final victory and we feast at his heavenly banquet" (UMH, Word and Table: Service I).

The invitation comes from Christ our Lord who "invites to his table *all* who love him, who earnestly repent of their sin and seek to live in peace with one another" (UMH, Word and Table: Service I, italics added). It is a table that looks at the whole world through the window of God's all-embracing love. Our table is waiting!

Questions for Journaling

- How have you experienced the Lord's Table as a table with a window on the world?

- When have you been tempted to limit your vision to the particular place in which you serve?
- How can you help the people you serve experience the universal love of God for the whole world?

Prayer

Pour out your Holy Spirit on us gathered here,
    and on these gifts of bread and wine.
Make them be for us the body and blood of Christ,
that we may be for the world the body of Christ, redeemed by
    his blood.

Renew our communion with your Church throughout the world,
and strengthen it in every nation and among every people
    to witness faithfully to your name.
By your Spirit make us one with Christ,
    one with each other, and one in ministry to all the world,
until Christ comes in final victory, and we feast at his heavenly
    banquet.

Through your Son Jesus Christ, with the Holy Spirit in your
    holy Church,
    all honor and glory is yours, almighty God, now and for
    ever. Amen.

—UMBOW, The Great Thanksgiving for World
                                Communion Sunday

Day 5: The Home We Dream

Read Hebrews 11:8-10; Psalm 84:5-9.

The Certificate of Naturalization hanging on our dining room wall declares "in the year of our Lord one thousand eight hundred and ninety-one, Fritz Hornbach, a native of Germany, exhibited a petition praying to be admitted a citizen of the United States." Fritz was my great-great-grandfather. He was among the "huddled masses yearning to breathe free" who immigrated to a place he had never seen with the dream of a better life.

I have a black-and-white photograph of Fritz's children and grandchildren, taken in 1918 on their little farm in the hills of Western Pennsylvania. They all look with stony seriousness toward the camera except my great-uncle Elwood. He's looking off toward something the rest don't see with a hint of a smile. He was the one who left the farm and went all the way to Pittsburgh, which had to be like immigrating to a new land. He lived on Mount Washington, looking out over the point where the Allegheny and Monongahela Rivers join and flow into the Ohio River, which carried pioneers to the West. For all I know, Elwood may have dreamed of going West himself.

People of biblical faith are spiritual descendants of an immigrant named Abraham. We follow people who were "looking forward to a city that has foundations, whose architect and builder is God" (Heb. 11:10). The psalmist writes that spiritual immigrants have pilgrimage in their hearts. They are grateful for what Frederick Buechner calls "the home [they] knew," but their hearts are set on "the home [they] dream of finding."[9] They live with a divine dissatisfaction with the way things are because they see the way things could be.

Around the time when Fritz Hornbach arrived at Ellis Island, Peggy McMichael's grandfather was a leading citizen in Tampa and a founding member of Hyde Park Methodist Episcopal Church, South. The church was the spiritual home she remembered, the place where she grew up, where she and her husband, Frank, were married and their children, grandchildren, and great-grandchildren were baptized. No one treasured the history of the church more than Peggy. But pilgrimage was in her heart. She was always looking to the future.

Peggy taught children's Sunday school long after others had passed the work on to younger leaders. She was drawn with a magnetic attraction to young couples for whom she and Frank became mentors and models of Christian marriage. She served on the committee that led the total renovation of the church buildings to serve a new generation. With gratitude for the home she remembered, she was always looking toward the home she dreamed.

Questions for Journaling

- What does it mean for you to be a pilgrim who has decided never to arrive?
- Are your life and faith more oriented to the home you remember or the home you dream?
- What is your vision of God's future for the ministry in which you serve?

Prayer

O God, who plants within me the longing for the home I dream, give me a divine dissatisfaction with the way things are so that I may be the active agent of the things you long for the world to become. Amen.

Week 4   Proclamation

Nothing that has happened to me since equals the power
and the glory that I sometimes felt when, in the middle
of a sermon, I knew that I was somehow, by some mira-
cle, really carrying, as they said, "the Word"—when the
church and I were one.

—James Baldwin (1924–1987)

A Fire in the Bones

Read Jeremiah 20:1-9.

If the word *ordinary* carries a sense of a regularly reoccurring event, then nothing is more ordinary for a pastor than preaching. I often say that for a preacher, Sundays come around with disturbing regularity. But if preaching is the way the Holy Spirit uses our spoken words to enable the written words of scripture to become the living Word in the congregation's experience, it becomes just about the most extraordinary thing a pastor is called to do.

When Lin-Manuel Miranda began recruiting the original Broadway cast for *Hamilton*, he knew that his friend Chris Jackson was the man to play George Washington. Jackson's towering, athletic physique and powerful baritone voice conveyed Washington's leadership during the Revolution and made Jackson a leader within the cast. Before each performance, he gathered the cast, musicians, and crew in a circle beneath the stage. He told them to hold hands and breathe deeply, and he gave what Miranda described as "half locker-room pep talk, half petition to the Almighty."[1] Jackson told the cast, "Let's be sure that no matter what happens out there . . . for the next two and half hours, this is the most important thing we'll do in our lives."[2] He would send the actors onto the stage with the hope that "everybody—in the audience, on the stage and in the orchestra pit—will leave the theater a better person than when they walked in."[3]

The image of that prayer circle beneath the stage led me to ask how often I go into worship with the sense of urgency the *Hamilton* cast carried onto the stage. Do I really believe that leading this particular congregation in worship and preaching this particular sermon at this particular time is the most important thing I can be doing with my life? Do I expect that in ways I can neither predict nor control we will all be better because we experienced it? Do I feel something like the fire in Jeremiah's bones that he could not put out? Would I say with Paul, "Woe to me if I do not proclaim the gospel!"? (1 Cor. 9:16, NRSV).

In the letter to the Romans, Paul asks the disturbing questions, "How can they have faith in someone they haven't heard of? And how can they hear without a preacher?" (Rom. 10:14). Ordinary pastors are called to answer that extraordinary question in ordinary congregations every time they stand up to preach. With all the seismic cultural shifts impacting our methods of communication, the proclamation of the good news remains at the center of our mission.

As one of the facilitators for the Institute of Preaching at Duke Divinity School, I review a pulpit full of sermons every year. One of the co-facilitators often asks, "Is there anything at stake here?" It's his way of asking, "Would this sermon make any discernible difference in the lives of the people who hear it? Is there any evidence that the preacher is a different person because he or she preached it? Does it matter?" In addition to working with preachers, we train a team of laypersons in their congregations to give helpful feedback to their preacher. Our involvement with these preachers and the congregational teams continues to confirm some basic convictions about preaching.

- *Preaching still makes a difference.* We've learned that both preachers and laypersons share a common conviction that preaching really matters. People still show up hoping to hear a word that will make a difference in the way they live during the week. If they don't, they have plenty of better things to do with their time. District Superintendents in The United Methodist Church report that when a new pastor is being appointed to a church, the first question a local-church committee asks is, "Can he or she preach?"

• *Preaching that makes a difference doesn't just happen.* A great artist once said that if people realized how much work it took to create his art, they would not think it was art anymore. Effective preaching is the result of consistent spiritual discipline, intense study, deep listening to the needs of the congregation, and old-fashioned hard work. Ernest Fremont Tittle (1885–1949) was one of America's leading preachers in the first half of the twentieth century. His words may be even more imperative today than when he first spoke them:

> Too many preachers are lying down on the job. Oh, to be sure, they are keeping busy, busy as bees, but not in the study. There, they merely dabble and dawdle. . . . a preacher who for any reason steps into [the] pulpit on Sunday morning unprepared . . . is not giving God a fair chance to speak to that congregation.[4]

• *Preaching that makes a difference happens in community.* Preaching that connects most deeply with people's lives happens in a particular place through a particular preacher who is deeply engaged in the lives of particular people. Duke homiletics professor Richard Lischer says we preach from "the embedded position . . . from pastoral participation in the life and death struggles of the baptized."[5]

• *Every preacher can become more effective than he or she currently is.* I often heard two questions about preaching in the later years of my pastoral ministry. Younger preachers would ask, "How did you stay fresh across twenty-two years in the same congregation?" First, I kept digging deeper into scripture. I found that I would not live long enough to exhaust it. Second, I watched the way the congregation and community kept changing around me. It took everything I could give to stay in touch with my people. The sermon I preached a decade ago would not be appropriate or adequate for the present moment.

The second question came from people in the congregation who asked, "How long did it take you to prepare that sermon?" My standard answer became, "About forty years." The proclamation of the Word demands that we never stop growing, learning, and finding a way to connect with the present moment. Rather, it grows out of a continued growth in a long obedience to the task.

In my first years as a pastor, I sent copies of my sermons to Dr. Charles Killian, my friend and homiletics professor, for his critique. With ruthless honesty he wrote on one sermon, "Puke... Puke... Puke! Largely gobbledygook. Lacks biblical or theological depth." I've kept that sermon in my file because he was correct. I'm a different preacher today than I was back then because of the continuing challenge to go deeper into the words of scripture and the lives of my people.

After more than four decades of preaching, I still approach the task with something like the urgency that sent the cast of *Hamilton* onto the stage. Preaching still feels like the most important thing I can do with my life. Every sermon is a new summons to proclaim the good news of what God has done in Christ and what God is calling us to be and do in our own time. Though I never faced the kind of opposition that confronted Jeremiah, I'm grateful that there is still "an intense fire . . . trapped in my bones" (Jer. 20:9) that I cannot put out.

Questions for Journaling

• How have you experienced something like Jeremiah's fire in your bones?
• When have you preached with the kind of urgency that Chris Jackson conveyed to the cast of *Hamilton*?
• What steps do you need to take to grow in your preaching?

Prayer

Lord, take my lips and speak through them;
take my mind and think through it;
take my heart and set it on fire. Amen.

—W. H. H. Aitken[6]

Day 1: Bloodstained Preaching

Read Acts 1:1-8; 4:1-22.

I've heard that the Gettysburg College library contains books soaked with the blood of soldiers who used the books as pillows while the Civil War battle raged around the tiny college campus. A current librarian (who also happens to be my niece) and a Gettysburg historian both report that they've never found any bloodstained books. It's evidently part of the fictional lore that has accumulated around the battle.

Nevertheless, the legend of the bloodstained books provides a powerful image that confirms the observation by Red Smith affirmed by Frederick Buechner: "All it takes to be a writer is to sit down at a keyboard, open a vein, and bleed."[7] In reviewing sermons, I often ask myself, *Is any of the preacher's blood in it? Is there evidence that what the preacher said flowed from deep inside the preacher's heart? Is the sermon a witness of what the preacher has experienced?*

At the Last Supper (see John 14:26-27) and again at the Ascension (see Acts 1:8), Jesus promises that by the power of the Holy Spirit his followers will be his witnesses. My lawyer friends taught me that in the courtroom the attorney argues the case, the jury decides the verdict, and the judge delivers the sentence. The only thing witnesses can do is report what they have seen, heard, or experienced. That's what Peter and John do when they are on trial for healing a lame man. They tell the court, "We can't stop speaking about what we have seen and heard" (Acts 4:20). Years later, John writes, "What we have seen and heard, we also announce it to you" (1 John 1:3). They are witnesses who preach out of their experience.

There is a time and place for arguing the truth of the gospel. Paul does it with limited success in Athens (see Acts 17:16-34), but his most powerful proclamations come from his experience. Like him, we are called to bear witness to the ways we have seen and heard the love of God that became flesh in Jesus becoming flesh in ordinary places and ordinary lives beginning with (but not limited to) our own. E. Stanley Jones wrote, "I do not sow a message apart from myself—I must be the message, embodied. Preaching a message apart from experience is the Word become word. . . . It is preaching the Word become flesh in Jesus and the Word become flesh in the proclaimer."[8]

But don't miss this! Peter and John's witness grows out of what they have seen and heard, but it points beyond their personal experience to the power of the risen Christ. Proclamation that makes a difference comes from us and through us but is ultimately not about us. The sermon has our blood soaked into it, but it points beyond us to the One whose love soaks through the whole of creation.

Questions for Journaling

- How does the legend of the bloodstained books speak to you?
- What difference does the role of the witness in the courtroom make for your preaching?
- How does your experience point toward Christ?

Prayer

Holy Spirit, Truth divine,
dawn upon this soul of mine;
Word of God and inward light,
wake my spirit, clear my sight.

Holy Spirit, Love divine,
glow within this heart of mine;
kindle every high desire;
perish self in thy pure fire.

—Samuel Longfellow (UMH, no. 465)

Day 2: "And to Preach the Word"

Read 1 Corinthians 1:18-31.

I've never forgotten the moment in 1970 when I placed my hand on the Bible and Bishop James Henley, in a raspy, Southern voice that sounded ancient to me at the time, spoke the traditional words of ordination, "Take thou authority to read the Holy Scriptures in the church of God and to preach the Word." I knew I was called to be a preacher. Though I've also served as a pastor, teacher, administrator, and denominational leader, my first calling was to "preach the Word." The challenge of connecting the truth of scripture with the people of the congregation never ceased to demand all the energy and creativity I could give.

The title *preacher* sometimes takes a well-deserved beating in our culture. There are more than enough corrupt, self-righteous, judgmental, greedy, manipulative, and downright heretical preachers to give anyone who is called to this work good reason to be cautious about the term. But in my experience as a preacher—and now, as a worshiper in the pew—I've witnessed that through "the foolishness of preaching" (1 Cor. 1:21, KJV) in the life of a warm-hearted, welcoming congregation, people are able to grasp the power of the gospel, are invited into a life of discipleship, and are challenged to participate in God's kingdom coming on earth as it is in heaven. Part of the foolishness in preaching is that our human weakness can reveal God's power. "We have this treasure in clay pots so that the awesome power belongs to God and doesn't come from us" (2 Cor. 4:7).

I found myself identifying with novelist Nickolas Butler's description of Charlie, the pastor of the dwindling congregation at St. Olaf's Lutheran Church. "His congregation adored him because they, too, sensed in him old faults and flaws. They saw in him themselves. There were no sharp corners left on Charlie—only rounded edges, like those smooth river stones a person plucks from the moving waters and keeps in their pocket."[9] One of the most meaningful compliments I received was when people would say, "You're the same person on Sunday morning that you are during the week."

Without doing my personal therapy in the pulpit, using my emotions to manipulate the congregation, setting myself up as a paragon of goodness, or revealing things in my life and relationships that needed to be resolved in private, I connected most deeply with my people when I humbly shared something of my own doubt, pain, hope, or joy. The sermons that had my blood in them became the sermons in which people could find themselves.

The mystery of preaching is that through our foolishness and weakness the wisdom and power of God can become a reality in the lives of our people.

Questions for Journaling

- What does it mean to you to be known as the "preacher"?
- How do you identify with Nickolas Butler's description of pastor Charlie?
- When has God used your weakness to reveal God's power?

Prayer

Lord, I am humbled by the realization that you would call
    someone like me to preach your Word.
Take my weakness and use it to reveal your power.
Take my doubt and use it to lead others to faith.
Take my fear and use it to build trust.
Take my failure and transform it into hope.
Take the gifts you have given me and make them your gift to
    others. Amen.

Day 3: What Makes Preaching Stick?

Read Romans 7:13–8:2.

Methodists founded a camp meeting at Bay View on the shore of Lake Michigan in 1875. It is now a historically designated community where generations of families have spent their summers in its Victorian cottages. On Sundays they hear a diverse assortment of speakers who preach in worship and teach in a forum during the week. Given the variety of preaching they have heard over the years, they were the perfect people to answer this question: "What makes preaching stick? What makes a sermon memorable?" I asked the questions to groups on two different occasions. Both groups named elements I expected: careful preparation, biblical depth, effective delivery, and memorable stories. But the number one quality on their lists was "authenticity." Their written comments included the following descriptions:

"Genuine."

"The preacher seemed like a real person."

"It felt like the preacher was one of us."

"Credible. They really believed what they preached."

"We get more than enough 'head' sermons. The ones that stick touch the heart."

Priest and theologian Ron Rolheiser makes a similar observation about the way Henri J. M. Nouwen connected with his hearers. Nouwen "deliberately chose to be radically honest; he could be deeply personal without being exhibitionistic; he could self-disclose without engaging in a spiritual striptease."[10] The apostle Paul pushes the boundaries on authenticity in uncovering his personal spiritual struggle to the folks in Rome. But he uses his struggle to announce the bold message of the gospel. The authenticity of his confession prepares the way for him to authentically declare, "There isn't any condemnation for those who are in Christ Jesus" (Rom. 8:1).

The irony in preaching is expressed by a friend who reminds me, "This is so *not* about us!" Preaching authentically rooted in scripture ultimately concerns what God has done, is doing, and intends to do in this world. But the authenticity of what God has done is revealed in the authenticity of our lives. I've dared to hope that my preaching would convey something of what Henry Ward Beecher (1813–1887) claimed as his theory of preaching.

> To have Christ so melted and dissolved in you that when you preach your own self you preach Him as Paul did: to have every part of you living and luminous with Christ, and then . . . to take everything that is in you all steeped in Jesus Christ, and to throw yourself with all your power upon a congregation—that has been my theory of preaching the Gospel.[11]

Questions for Journaling

- Where have you experienced authenticity in preaching?
- How much of yourself are you willing share in your preaching?
- What spiritual disciplines do you need to develop so that Christ will be "melted and dissolved in you"?

Prayer

O God, whose perfect love was perfectly revealed in Jesus, I offer my imperfections to you. Save me from selfish pride or spiritual arrogance. May I be so steeped in the words and way of your Son that my life and my words will be luminous with his love, humility, compassion, and peace. May the Word that became flesh in Jesus become flesh again through me. Amen.

Day 4: Speak What We Feel

Read Jeremiah 8:19–9:2.

The most emotionally powerful song in *Hamilton*, "It's Quiet Uptown," follows the death of Alexander Hamilton's son Philip. Angelica sings what any parent who has buried a child knows: "There are moments that the words don't reach. There is suffering too terrible to name."[12] Watching the grief-stricken parents, the company sings about how Alexander and Eliza are doing the "unimaginable." But in the song, Alexander and Eliza move through unimaginable pain to equally unimaginable grace.

The scene left me speechless, just the way I often feel speechless when I enter into moments of unimaginable loss as a pastor. They are times when words can't touch the pain, and all we can offer is compassionate silence. And yet, a preacher is called to do the unimaginable: to put words around feelings and experiences that are too large for words to contain. In these moments I often turned to Shakespeare's closing lines in *King Lear*:

The weight of this sad time we must obey.
Speak what we feel, not what we ought to say.[13]

In moments that words won't touch, we might be tempted to reach for things we ought to say and end up with weak words that can't carry the freight of the moment—pious platitudes or simplistic slogans that skim across the surface of the pain without acknowledging its depth. Though we cannot go all the way to the bottom of another person's loss, we can at least name it and walk with them to the edge of the darkness.

Jeremiah listens to the weeping of his people and gives voice to the question that is buried beneath the surface of their suffering: "Isn't the LORD in Zion?" (Jer. 8:19). He identifies with their desperation—"Because my people are crushed, I am crushed" (Jer. 8:21)—and pours out his own grief—"If only my head were a spring of water, and my eyes a fountain of tears" (Jer. 9:1). He also lifts the word of hope: "I am the LORD who acts with kindness, justice, and righteousness in the world" (Jer. 9:24).

When the firstborn son of one of the most faithful families in my congregation committed suicide, I was called as their pastor and friend to speak to the unimaginable. Everyone knew how he died, but the friends who spoke during the memorial service told pleasant stories that never acknowledged the grief hanging like a rain-soaked blanket over the congregation. They said what they knew they ought to say. It was my task to speak the truth and to offer a word of grace that would point through the darkness toward the hope of healing and peace.

An almost palpable feeling of release spread through a congregation that had been holding its corporate breath when I spoke what we all felt, gave voice to the questions that were being held prisoner in our minds, and named the grace that was available to us. In a time of unimaginable pain, we experienced "grace too powerful to name" and claimed the unimaginable hope of resurrection.

When we face the unimaginable, may we preach what we feel, not what we think we ought to say.

Questions for Journaling

- When have you experienced unimaginable loss or pain?
- How do you find grace in the painful places in your life?
- What is the word of grace you can offer to others?

Prayer

O Love that wilt not let me go,
I rest my weary soul in thee;
I give thee back the life I owe,
That in thine ocean depths its flow
may richer, fuller be.

O Joy that seekest me through pain,
I cannot close my heart to thee;
I trace the rainbow thru the rain,
and feel the promise is not vain
that morn shall tearless be.

O Cross that liftest up my head,
I dare not ask to fly from thee;
I lay in dust life's glory dead,
and from the ground there blossoms red
life that shall endless be.

—George Matheson (UMH, no. 480)

Day 5: A Time for Shouting

Read Isaiah 58:1-14; Romans 8:1-30.

It was Ash Wednesday 2018. The newspaper's front-page photograph of a grief-stricken woman holding a sobbing girl in her arms is engraved in my memory. The anguish in her face said everything that could be said after seventeen students died in the school shooting at Marjory Stoneman Douglas High School in Parkland, Florida, another of the shootings that happen with horrendous regularity in our gun-saturated nation. I couldn't help but notice the ash-black sign of the cross on her forehead.

I immediately imagined that the pastor who applied those ashes earlier in the day, saying, "Remember that you are dust and to dust you will return," never thought of death like this. The voice within us that shouts, "This is not the way it should be!" is nothing less than the Spirit of God shouting in the depths of our souls with groans too deep for words (see Romans 8:26).

The Ash Wednesday scripture readings included Isaiah 58:1, where God commands, "Shout loudly; don't hold back; raise your voice like a trumpet!" God mocks a people who seek God *as if* they are "a nation that acted righteously" (Isa. 58:2). God blows off their phony piety and their smarmy self-righteousness by calling them to direct action that demonstrates their faithfulness to God's way of doing things. I have no doubt that God shares our tears, feels our pain, and hears our prayers. But I also know that "thoughts and prayers" are not enough. God must be fed up with our moments of silence, our half-staffed flags, and our empty rhetoric about mental illness and gun safety. It is time for righteous anger and a call to redemptive action.

I feel called to shout that it is time for people who believe the Bible to demand reasonable gun control laws; to increase funding for school guidance counselors, social workers, and teachers who are called to teach our children, not to die for them; to reinstate restrictions on gun purchases by people with a record of mental illness or criminal violence; to stop the unregulated sale of weapons at gun shows; and to seriously question voting for politicians who receive money from the gun lobby.

There is a time for shouting. There are times when proclaiming a biblical vision for our world demands a prophetic word of judgment and hope that confronts the economic, political, racial, and social injustice of our time. The Lord promises Isaiah that when we turn our prayers into faithful action our "light will shine in the darkness, and [our] gloom will be like the noon" (Isa. 58:10). Perhaps then—and only then—we will deserve to be called "Mender of Broken Walls, Restorer of Livable Streets" (Isa. 58:12).

If we are faithful to the Word made flesh in Jesus, there will be a time for shouting. In those times our calling is not only to comfort the afflicted but also to afflict the comfortable with God's Word of justice and grace.

Questions for Journaling

- When have you heard God calling you to shout the prophetic word of justice and grace?
- When have you been paralyzed by fear and avoided preaching a prophetic word?
- How can you be more faithful to speak God's Word to the social, political, and economic realities of our world?

Prayer

Give us courage, O Lord, to stand up and be counted, to stand up for those who cannot stand up for themselves, to stand up for ourselves when it is needful. . . . Let us fear nothing more than we fear Thee. Let us love nothing more than we love Thee. . . . Let us have no other god before Thee, whether nation or party or state or church. Let us seek no other peace but the peace which is Thine, and make us its instruments, opening our eyes and our ears and our hearts, so that we should know always what work of peace we may do for Thee.

—Alan Paton (1903–1988)[14]

Week 5   Perseverance

I don't want religion as comfort, but as adequacy. I don't want God to hold my hand, I want [God] to strengthen my arm that I might reach out a helping hand to others.
—E. Stanley Jones (1884–1973)

When the Going Gets Tough

Read Matthew 10:16-25; 2 Corinthians 4:1-12.

The high school locker room was never a comfortable place for me as a skinny, athletically challenged adolescent. But I remember a motivational sign hanging on the wall that read, "When the going gets tough, the tough get going." It's a good motto to hang on the wall of our souls because none of us is immune to difficulties; no one is excluded. Sooner or later, in one way or another, life gets tough for everyone. Among the required equipment for the journey through Ordinary Time is perseverance, a tenacious determination to hang in there through whatever comes. Gil Rendle describes it as "steadfastness . . . the steady pursuit of the 'why' that lies at the center of our communities of faith."[1] It's what Paul had in mind when he wrote the following: "We are experiencing all kinds of trouble, but we aren't crushed. We are confused, but we aren't depressed. We are harassed, but we aren't abandoned. We are knocked down, but we aren't knocked out" (2 Cor. 4:8-9).

Some tough times come like a hurricane making its laborious way across the Atlantic Ocean and into the Gulf of Mexico. We have time to make evacuation plans; cover storefront windows with plywood; stock up on food, water, and batteries before the power goes out. We still have to withstand the fury of the storm, the darkness of the night, the pounding rain, the locomotive sound of the wind; but at least we are prepared for it.

Some tough times take us by surprise like an earthquake that sends unexpected shock waves along the California coastline.

Suddenly and without warning foundations begin to shake, windows explode, walls give way, and ceilings crash in.

Some are the inescapable effect of racial, social, or economic injustice; some are simply the result of time or aging; and some, if we tell the truth, are the result of our own mistakes. However it happens, sooner or later the going will get tough, particularly if we are faithful to the gospel in the long obedience of ministry.

Prophets, like Jeremiah or Esther, who are sent to announce God's judgment and hope inevitably face resistance or opposition. Reformers, like John the Baptist, who are commissioned to make crooked places straight and rough places plain find that building the highway involves breaking resistant ground and moving stubborn rocks. Followers of the risen Christ who bear witness to God's new creation soon discover that there is always pain for the mother when new life is born. Leaders, like Martin Luther King Jr., who believe there is a moral arc in the universe that bends toward justice and who want to invest their energy in the bending inevitably confront resistant forces determined to bend the arc in the opposite direction.

It's not as if we should be surprised by this reality. Jesus clearly warns his disciples that he is sending them like sheep among wolves and that they will face opposition. But he also promises, "Whoever stands firm until the end will be saved" (Matt. 10:22). The question is not *will* tough times come, but *how* will we face them and *what* can we learn that will carry us through?

Father James Martin, the highly respected and widely read editor-at-large of *America* magazine, shared seven lessons he learned that resonate with my own experience.[2]

1. "You can't know everything." I had to accept that I don't have all the answers. Sometimes the challenges are too complex, the conflict too intense, the opposition too strong, and the pain too deep for simplistic responses that, like the house built on sand, won't withstand the storm. Father Martin wrote, "You study hard, take your work seriously and give yourself fully to your ministry. But you're not going to be able to answer

every question, solve every problem, meet every ministerial challenge."

2. "You can't do everything." This has been a hard lesson for me. I ended up with a classic midlife crisis because I burned out both physically and spiritually by trying to meet every need and do everything I thought had to be done. I learned the hard way to take Paul's advice not to think of myself more highly than I ought to think but to have a sane estimate of what I can and cannot do (see Romans 12:3).

3. "You can do some things." Reflecting on 9/11, Father Martin concluded, "I would have been overwhelmed or paralyzed if I thought I had to do everything at Ground Zero. Instead, I did what I could: the ministry of presence." No matter how difficult the situation, there is always something we can do to make a Christlike difference.

4. "You can always learn something new." I continue to be challenged by the memory of two aging heroes in my last congregation. Both were approaching ninety, both facing the physical challenges of aging, but they never stopped learning new things, reading new books, wrestling with new ideas and challenging me to do the same. If I ever grow up, I want to be like them.

5. "You can't be liked by everyone." This has been another tough lesson for me. I'm grateful for a mentor and friend who loved me enough to say my need to be loved was too great. He helped me let go of the illusion that everyone would like me. Being faithful to the gospel will inevitably lead toward rejection. It happened to Jesus in his hometown (see Luke 4:14-30). What makes us think it won't happen to us?

6. "You can be like Jesus." Why is something so obvious so obviously difficult? We are called to be like Jesus: to allow the mind, attitude, and perspective that was in Christ to be at work in us (see Philippians 2:5-11); to allow the fruits of the Spirit—"love, joy, peace, patience, kindness, goodness, faithfulness,

gentleness, and self-control" (Gal. 5:22-23)—to grow in us. Father Martin said, "You can always be kind."

7. "You were called by God into the ministry." The lessons Father Martin and I learned take us back to the beginning of our ministry. God called *me*, which means that God intends to use *me* with all my strengths and weaknesses as a part of God's work in this world. During one of the toughest days of my ministry, I received a letter from one of my closest friends in which he simply wrote, "Just be Jim. That will be enough."

In difficult times, Father Martin calls us to remember this: "At your baptism, God called you into the church by name. And in your ministry, God made a further call. . . . When things get tough for me, I think of . . . those disciples Jesus called. . . . And I am sure that at the worst times they . . . remembered who called them."

During a recent tough time for me, a South African friend encouraged me by writing, "The things we do not choose can be terrifying, but we can, in the midst of it, remain whole and at peace." That's the tenacious power of perseverance.

Questions for Journaling

• How have difficult times come for you? As a hurricane or as an earthquake?
• What does Jesus' promise to the disciples mean to you?
• Which of Father Martin's lessons resonate with your experience?

Prayer

May God bless us with discomfort at easy answers, half-truths and superficial relationships, so that we may live from deep within our hearts.

May God bless us with anger at injustice, oppression and exploitation of people, so that we may work for justice, freedom and peace.

May God bless us with tears to shed for those who suffer with
pain, rejection, starvation and war, so that we may reach
out our hand to comfort them and turn their pain to joy. . . .
May God bless us with enough foolishness to believe that we
can make a difference in this world, so that we can do what
others claim cannot be done: to bring justice and kindness
to all our children and the poor.
In God's great grace, we say Amen—so be it!
                —South African Benediction (Anonymous)[3]

Day 1: Ministry in the Whirlpool of Change

Read Psalm 36:5-9; 37:37.

Change is as difficult as it is inevitable. Leading change is even harder. Pastors are often asked to produce change, but just as often they face resistance when they do it. Learning to live with and lead through change is a critical factor in the long and joyful obedience of ministry.

Downton Abbey fans remember that the underlying theme of the series was how people dealt with change, most of it unexpected, much of it unwelcome, and all of it beyond the power of the Crawleys and their servants to control, although the Dowager Countess did everything she could to resist it. The entire household depended upon the stability with which Lord Grantham upstairs and Mr. Carson downstairs maintained their core values while adapting to the whirlpool of change that swirled around them.

In one poignant episode, Thomas Barrow, the under-butler, interviewed for a position in a once grand but now crumbling old house where a bitter old man reminisced about the days gone by and dreamed that if he held out long enough, those days would return. But we know they never will. Sadly, it reminded me of some churches I've observed.

It's an understatement to say that we serve in a time of seismic cultural change. While change carries the risk of loss and change for change's sake is a dangerous fantasy, the "good ol' days"—many of which were not as good as we remember them—are not coming back. In times like these, the test of our ministry will be the stability of our leadership in dealing with change. While the relentless winds of change could cause us to become defensive, angry, or afraid, our lives can bear witness to the persevering love and faithfulness of God that T. S. Eliot called "the still point of the turning world."[4]

There are gifts from the past that we need to preserve—traditions that provide ballast to keep our ship afloat in the storm, core values that stand the test of time. For us as it was for the folks at Downton, it's about drawing on deeper resources of love and faith. It's about honoring tradition without being imprisoned by it and about reshaping our traditions for a new and different time. James Baldwin wrote, "To accept one's past—one's history—is not the same thing as drowning in it; it is learning how to use it."[5]

Questions for Journaling

- How have you experienced both the desire for and resistance to change?
- What are some gifts of the past that can guide you through change?
- How can you keep God as "the still point" of your ministry?

Prayer

O God, whose love is unchanged by time or circumstances, sometimes I would like to go back to the way things once were or hold onto the way things are right now. In the whirlpool of change, give me confidence in your unchanging love that I may face the future unafraid, through Jesus Christ who is the same forever and ever. Amen.

Day 2: "I Beg to Differ"

Read Hebrews 12:1-15.

The 1986 World Methodist Conference in Nairobi, Kenya, was no ordinary time for me. It was, in fact, an extraordinary and spiritually formative moment for my life and ministry. During some of the darkest days in the struggle against apartheid, Archbishop Desmond Tutu told the conference that God enlists us to participate in transforming "the ugliness of this world . . . into the laughter and the joy, the compassion and the goodness, the love and the peace, the justice and the reconciliation . . . to make the kingdoms of this world to become the kingdom of our God and of his Christ."[6] When there was little external evidence to support his vision of freedom and justice, the courageous Archbishop declared, "Victory is assured! Because the death and resurrection of our Savior Jesus Christ declares forever and ever that light has overcome darkness, that life has overcome death, that joy and laughter and peace and compassion and justice and caring and sharing, all and more have overcome their counterparts . . . we are seeing the fulfillment of this wonderful vision in the revelation of Saint John the Divine."[7]

A day later, Peter Storey, then the pastoral leader of Central Methodist Mission in Johannesburg, called on the conference to celebrate the victory that was yet to be accomplished. "Because Jesus breaks the walls; because Jesus gives a liberty that none can take away; because His Church will be kept faithful to hope. . . . Apartheid is doomed!"[8] Peter described the large, white candle surrounded by barbed wire that stood on the altar at Central Methodist Mission. In worship they lit the candle as they called the names of people who had been arrested or were in prison, prayed for freedom, and committed themselves again to be the agents of God's justice and peace in their land. The candle symbolized the words of the Indian theologian and poet Samuel Rayan who imagines a candle saying to the darkness, "I beg to differ."[9]

That extraordinary time in Nairobi began a relationship with the Methodists of South Africa that continues to exert a transformative influence in my life. It led to my first visit to Johannesburg when I had the humbling privilege of lighting that special candle in worship. It resulted in ongoing connections with faithful pastors and lay persons who continue to demonstrate a tenacious commitment to the vision of the kingdom of God becoming a reality on earth as it is already fulfilled in heaven. They have modeled the persevering faith and tenacious witness described by the writer of Hebrews, which call me to "strengthen [my] drooping hands and weak knees" (12:12) for the long obedience of ministry.

Questions for Journaling

+ How do the words of Desmond Tutu and Peter Storey speak to your life and faith?
+ When have you seen the light in the darkness that begs to differ?
+ How have you experienced the kind of perseverance the writer of Hebrews describes?

Prayer

Our Father in Heaven, give us the long view of our work and our world.

Help us to see that it is better to fail in a cause that will ultimately succeed than to succeed in a cause that will ultimately fail.

Guide us how to work and then teach us how to wait. O Lord, we pray in the name of Jesus, who was never in a hurry. Amen.

—Peter Marshall (1902–1949)[10]

Day 3: Sacred Resistance

Read Ephesians 6:10-20.

I love the United Methodist liturgy for baptism because it dares to tell the truth. I confess that in looking into the adoring faces of the parents and grandparents of a newborn child I am almost reluctant to ask the following questions:

> Do you renounce the spiritual forces of wickedness, reject the evil powers of this world, and repent of your sin? Do you accept the freedom and power God gives you to resist evil, injustice, and oppression in whatever forms they present themselves? (*имн*, Baptismal Covenant II)

When I stood beside the font as a parent and grandparent, wickedness, evil, injustice, and oppression were not the first things on my mind. But the church doesn't protect us from the truth. This is the world into which this child has been born; these are the evils this child will face. The baptismal covenant calls us to resist those evils even as it promises us the power of God to overcome them. Paul is equally honest about the evils we face when he calls us to put on "the full armor of God" so that we can be prepared to "stand [our] ground on the evil day and after [we] have done everything possible to still stand" (Eph. 6:13).

My friend and colleague Ginger Gaines-Cirelli practices Paul's words as she leads the people of Foundry United Methodist Church in Washington, D.C., in "sacred resistance." She reaffirms the commitment we make in baptism when she writes that "sacred resistance is at the heart of our *being*, not just our *doing*. . . . Our inward posture centers on God and resists all that is *not* God, resists all that is counter to the ways of God revealed through Jesus. . . . It is 'sacred' because it is driven by God at work in and through us. It is 'sacred' because it is grounded in God's vision of wholeness."[11]

This passage from Ephesians was our class verse at the small, Methodist-rooted college where I graduated fifty years ago. Back then I had no idea what it would mean "to resist evil in its day of power." In my naive idealism, I didn't know there would be times when I would be brought to a standstill and the only thing left to do was to stand my ground. I had not experienced the sustaining power of hope that Ginger describes as "the assurance that no matter what mess we humans make of things, no matter how lost we become, no matter how much damage we do to one another and to the creation, God has been, is, and will be at work to restore, renew, and resurrect."[12]

A pastor friend who was facing a difficult conflict in his congregation found strength to stand when his young son said, "It's okay, Daddy. Be good and be brave."

Questions for Journaling

- How have you experienced the "spiritual forces of wickedness"?
- How can you identify with Paul's words to the Ephesians?
- What will it mean for you to practice "sacred resistance" in your ministry and leadership?

Prayer

Soldiers of Christ, arise,
and put your armor on,
strong in the strength which God supplies,
thru his eternal Son;
strong in the Lord of Hosts,
and in his mighty power,
who in the strength of Jesus trusts

is more than conqueror.

From strength to strength go on;
wrestle, and fight, and pray;
tread all the powers of darkness down
and win the well-fought day.
Still let the Spirit cry
in all his soldiers, "Come!"
Till Christ the Lord descends from high
and take the conquerors home.

—Charles Wesley (UMH, no. 513)

Day 4: Clarify Your Calling

Read Jeremiah 1:4-19; Luke 4:14-21.

When I was appointed to lead a ninety-three-year-old congregation in a rapidly changing urban center, a perceptive lay person, sensing the challenge before me and the resistance I would face, gave me a recorded series of lectures by Edwin Friedman based on his groundbreaking book *Generation to Generation: Family Process in Church and Synagogue.* I had no idea how important those lectures would become for my leadership.

Friedman taught the importance of "self-differentiation," which includes clarity about one's own principles, personal vulnerability, persistence in confronting resistance, and regulation of emotions when encountering sabotage. My personal principles and the congregational vision became clearer in and through the struggle we faced. I confess that I was not always able to demonstrate the self-regulation of emotions Friedman described. But I learned that what the congregation needed was a leader who would hold onto a few core values with tenacious certainty, the way sailors steered their ships through rough water by holding firmly to the tiller.

Jeremiah is a biblical example of Friedman's principle. His prophetic ministry begins with a clear sense of who he is and what God is calling him to do and be. That clarity sustains him through the conflict, pain, and opposition he faces. In the same way, Jesus finds clarity about his calling during his time in the wilderness and declares his personal principles and ministry vision in Nazareth.

When Peter Storey was appointed to Central Methodist Mission in 1964, he knew that it would need to be similar to the "confessing church" in Nazi Germany. He settled on four principles that guided him for the rest of his life. He called them the lifeline that held him fast when he feared he would lose his grip.

• "To be a truth-teller, to proclaim the truth without fear and expose the lie of apartheid."
• "To bind up the broken, siding with the victims of injustice wherever I found them."
• "To try and 'live the alternative', seeking to be a visible contradiction of the apartheid state's cruel segregation practices and offering a picture of God's alternative."
• "To work in non-violent, Christ-like ways to bring in a new dispensation of justice, equity and peace."[13]

Perseverance in the long obedience of ministry grows out of deep clarity about who we are and who God is calling us to be.

Questions for Journaling

• How does Friedman's description of "self-differentiation" speak to you?
• How can you identify with Jeremiah's call or Jesus' declaration in Nazareth?
• What core principles or convictions guide your ministry?

Prayer

Grant, O God, that in all time of our testing we may know your presence and obey your will; that . . . we may with integrity and courage accomplish what you give us to do, and endure what you give us to bear; through Jesus Christ our Lord, who lives and reigns with you and the Holy Spirit, one God, for ever and ever. Amen.
—Edward Bouverie Pusey (1800–1882)[14]

Day 5: The Best of Things in the Worst of Times

Read Psalm 37.

The inscription over the door of the Chapel of the Holy Trinity at Staunton Harold near Leicestershire, England, bears witness to the perseverance of Sir Robert Shirley. Shirley's loyalty to the Church of England resulted in his imprisonment in the Tower of London, where he died in 1656.

In the year 1653
when all thinges Sacred were throughout ye nation
Either demolisht or profaned
Sir Robert Shirley, Barronet,
Founded this Church;
Whose singular praise it is
to have done the best things in ye worst times,
and
hoped them in the most calamitous.
The righteous shall be had in everlasting remembrance.[15]

Psalm 37 was written for people who feel they are living in "the worst of times." The "spiritual forces of wickedness" and "evil powers of this world" are apparently getting their way. Sooner or later, we all share that experience. We ask, "What can we do?" The imperative verbs in the psalm help me answer that question (italics added).

* v. 3: *Trust* the Lord and *do good*; *live* in the land, and *farm* faithfulness.
* v. 5: *Commit* your way to the Lord! *Trust* him!
* v. 7: *Be still* before the Lord, and *wait* for him.
* v. 8: *Let go* of anger and *leave rage* behind.
* v. 27: *Turn away* from evil! *Do good!*
* v. 37: *Observe* those who have integrity.

The psalmist is confident that although evil will have its day, God's goodness ultimately will prevail. The writer hears God laughing at the evildoer who, in the words of Shakespeare's Macbeth, "struts and frets his hour upon the stage, and then is heard no more." The psalm reverberates with confidence in what one statement of faith calls "the final triumph of righteousness and . . . the life everlasting" (UMH, no. 884).

In 1991, Roland Rink heard God calling him to leave a successful career as a telecommunications executive to give birth to Africa Upper Room Ministries, a ministry he led for eighteen years. When I asked Roland how he persevered across the years, he described his daily practice to remember what he calls "The 4 Ls". Like the psalmist, he listed imperative verbs that have sustained him:

* *Listen* to God through scripture, prayer, meditation.
* *Leap* in faith each day, each hour, each moment.
* *Leave* it to God, remembering that God is with us. We are not alone.
* *Look* at what God has done as the evidence that God is working for good for us always.

That's the kind of persevering faith that will enable us to do the best of things in the worst of times and to continue to live with confident hope.

Questions for Journaling

* Who have you known who has demonstrated the persevering faith of Sir Robert Shirley?
* How do the imperative verbs in Psalm 37 speak to you?

• What specific practices will enable you to do the best of things in the worst of times?

Prayer

Grant, O most gracious God, that I may carry with me through this day's life the remembrance of the suffering and death of Jesus Christ my Lord. . . .

Give me grace . . . to understand the meaning of such afflictions and disappointments as I am called upon to endure. . . . Give me a stout heart to bear my own burdens. Give me a willing heart to bear the burdens of others. Give me a believing heart to cast all burdens upon Thee. Amen.

—John Baillie (1886–1960)[16]

Week 6   Promise

A Christian leader. . . . faces the world with eyes full of expectation, with the expertise to take away the veil that covers its hidden potential.

—Henri J. M. Nouwen (1932–1996)

What Comes Next?

Read Hebrews 11:8-12, 39-40; Luke 9:21-27.

King George III is the comic character in the musical *Hamilton*. When the revolutionaries declare their independence, he sings "You'll Be Back," confident that everything will return to the way things were before the revolution. And if they don't come back, he promises to bring them back by force. After the British surrender in Yorktown, his song becomes a question: "What Comes Next?"

I remembered King George when I read Gil Rendle's disturbingly accurate description of the post-WWII era as an "aberrant time" for American church growth. He names the unique reasons that it was a build-it-and-they-will-come era. Congregations added staff and built larger buildings for their expanding programs. Following corporate models, the mainline denominations developed large bureaucracies and equally large buildings to house them. The Interchurch Center at 475 Riverside Drive in New York City became the God-box on the Hudson for church agencies. No wonder my parents are among those called "the Builder Generation." Like King George, many of us would like to believe those days might come back again. Some of us are baffled that they haven't. But Rendle simply says, "There is no going back because the 'back' that is remembered doesn't exist anymore."[1]

My last pastoral appointment was a short-term stint as the interim lead pastor at First United Methodist Church in Orlando. In the era of explosive growth, the congregation built a soaring new sanctuary with a steeple that rose above the downtown skyline. But as taller buildings going up around it have dwarfed the steeple, the membership and attendance at First Church have declined. Meanwhile, many faithful folks have held onto the hope that it will all come back. On my first Sunday, one elder saint spoke a word that contained more truth than she realized when she said, "I just don't understand why people don't come to church anymore."

As a result of such shifts, leaders in my generation are asking the following questions:

• What comes next?
• What does it mean to be the body of Christ on this side of a cultural revolution?
• What happens when Ordinary Time isn't *ordinary* in the way we remember it?

The next generations of young leaders are asking deeper questions:

• Will the church in which I am ordained still be here as a place for me to serve?
• How will we bear witness to Christ in a culture that no longer shares a common set of religious values?
• How can we tell "the old, old story of Jesus and his love" to people who have no Christian memory or whose images of the church are tainted by headlines of political partisanship, LGBTQ exclusion, and moral scandal?
• What comes next?

Realizing that people of biblical faith have been in similar situations before me helps when I feel overwhelmed by these questions. These are the kind of questions the children of Israel asked after crossing the Red Sea. Released from the orderly oppression of slavery, how will they order their lives in a disorderly wilderness? With their identity no longer defined by Pharaoh, who will they be as people whose identity is defined by their relationship with God? When Moses is no longer there to lead them, who will show them the way? What comes next?

The early Christians face similar questions on the other side of Pentecost. They wrestle with questions they never have asked before. How will they live together in the ordinary days following the extraordinary experience of Easter and Pentecost? Who will lead them into the unknown world beyond the boundaries of Judaism? How will they bear witness to the coming of the kingdom of God in a world dominated by the Roman Empire? What comes next?

A biblical, one-word answer to those questions could be *promise*. We live into the promise of God's future. We're always "standing on the promises of God." Abraham heads to an unknown land with nothing but the promise that he will become the father of a great nation. Moses confronts Pharaoh with the promise that the Lord will be with him and will set his people free. Mary offers herself to God's purpose in the promise that she will give birth to the Savior. Jesus goes to the cross with the promise that he will be raised on the third day. Mary Magdalene runs from the empty tomb with the promise that the risen Christ will go before her. The disciples wait in Jerusalem with the promise of the coming of the Holy Spirit. John endures incarceration on Patmos with the promise that one day the kingdoms of this earth will become the kingdom of God.

Whatever comes next, we stand on the promises of God. We are called to live today in ways that are consistent with the way things will be when God's kingdom comes. We dare to believe that we play an active part in its coming. But it isn't easy. Living into God's promise in the future always involves dying to something in the past.

After reading the first draft of this week's study, a pastoral colleague in South Africa wrote that one thing that keeps her going is the awareness that we are bound to Christ when we die to ourselves and say yes again and again to Jesus. She observed that the ability of leaders like Peter Storey and Desmond Tutu to see beyond what is to the possibility of what could be grew out of their being shaped by dying to self and living into Christ over and over again.

Here's the central paradox of the Christian life: "All who want to save their lives will lose them. But all who lose their lives because of me will save them" (Luke 9:24). Good Friday and Easter are not just extraordinary events we remember from the past; death and resurrection define the spiritual pattern for the extraordinary way we are called to live. Paul claims that truth when he writes, "I have been crucified with Christ and I no longer live, but Christ lives in me" (Gal. 2:20).

The journey through ordinary time into the extraordinary promise of God's future leads inexorably to the cross where we die to old ways of living, thinking, and being in order to be raised again to the new life to which Christ calls us. In the ordinary days of our own ministry, we will discover what it means to die to self and live for Christ over and over again. We are not only "standing on" but also "living into" the promises of God.

Questions for Journaling

- When have you asked what happens next?
- How have you felt the promise of God for your ministry?
- What will it mean for you to live into God's promise for your life?

Prayer

Eternal God, give me faith to trust your promise in the present
    so that I can participate in what you intend for the future.
Guide my feet to follow where you are leading.
Strengthen my hands to do your will.
Enlarge my heart to receive all that you have for me,
through Jesus Christ who is the fulfillment of your promise.
    Amen.

Day 1: The Other Side of Ordinary Time

Read 1 Corinthians 1:1-9; Philippians 1:1-6.

On the other side of Ordinary Time, we enter the season of Advent. The liturgical calendar suggests that we journey through the ordinary days of our ministry in the promise of something yet to come.

Advent is more than just the church's way of capitalizing on the marketing for Christmas that begins earlier every year. It's the season when we wait for the fulfillment of God's promise that was revealed in Jesus. It's more than a nostalgic return to Christmases past. It is a season of hope as we look forward to what God will do in the future because we know what God has done in the past. We live into the "not yet" of the kingdom of God that is to come because we are part of the kingdom that has "already" come among us in Christ.

The scripture readings for the First Sunday of Advent always point toward the final coming of Christ. Advent begins with eschatology, the end-without-an-ending toward which God's redeeming work in history moves relentlessly. The beginning of the new liturgical year directs our vision to the final beginning of God's redemptive renewal of all creation.

I confess that some years I skipped the eschatological readings and jumped ahead to the Christmas Gospel. I also confess that mainline preachers have often left eschatology to folks who read Daniel and Revelation as if they were a schedule of coming events for the twenty-first century. Given the "end times" talk in the culture around us, there might be good reasons to skip the subject altogether. There are, however, better reasons to dig deeper into the scripture texts and reclaim the promise we are going somewhere and that the God who called us into this ministry will strengthen us to the end.

We make our way through ordinary time assured that "the one who began a good work among you will bring it to completion by the day of Jesus Christ" (Phil. 1:6, NRSV). We are called to live now in ways that model the way the world will be when "the kingdom of the world has become the kingdom of our Lord" (Rev. 11:15). We serve with our eyes fixed on eternity. The purpose of biblical eschatology is not to provide detailed information on the dimensions of heaven or to set a calendar for the end of time but to inspire us with a sense of direction for the way we live right now. What we believe about the future shapes our life in the present.

In ordinary days when our ordinary ministry in ordinary places doesn't seem to be making much of a difference, the reminder that we are participating in the yet-to-be-fulfilled promise of God's kingdom can be the assurance that strengthens us for the long obedience of ministry.

Questions for Journaling

- How does your understanding of eschatology affect your ministry?
- What difference does it make for you to make your way through ordinary time with the promise of Advent?
- How does your ministry participate in the coming of God's kingdom?

Prayer

O eternal God, open my eyes to see the way my ministry now is a part of your kingdom that is yet to come. Enable me to trust the promise that having begun a good work in my life, you will see it to completion in the day of Christ. Amen.

Day 2: A Defiant Joy

Read Philippians 4:1-9.

E very day's headlines provide ample evidence of the pervasive power of evil around us. Sam Keen, best known for his insights into the personal and spiritual lives of men, warned that if we only pay attention to those headlines, we can become "hypnotized by evil and either turn aside in despair . . . or become fanatical warriors . . . [who] burn out and give those around them heartburn."[2] Keen advised that the only way "to get through this world alive" (and I would add the only way to thrive in the long obedience of ministry) is to "care until our hearts break and cram our lives full of enjoyment."[3]

Unfortunately, I've known pastors who fit Keen's description of men in our culture when he wrote, "If I were asked to diagnose the spiritual disease of modern men [pastors], . . . I would focus on our lack of joy. Most of the men [pastors] I know are decent, serious, and hard-working, and would like to make the world a better place. What they are not is juicy, sensual, and fun."[4]

Consider this a call for a juicier, more joyful ministry!

The Third Sunday in Advent is called *Gaudate*, the Latin word meaning "rejoice." It was originally a joyful pause in a season of repentance. The scripture readings include Paul's imperative command: "Rejoice in the Lord always; again I will say, Rejoice" (Phil. 4:4, NRSV). Paul is writing from a prison cell when he calls for joy that is neither dependent on nor defeated by external circumstances; joy that flows out of the heart of a person who has found a deep, abiding trust in the goodness of God; joy that is not a naive denial of what the world has come to but a defiant confidence in what has come to the world in Jesus Christ. It is the joy that the writer of Proverbs celebrates in the strong, faithful woman who "laughs at the time to come" (Prov. 31:25, NRSV). Thomas Merton called it "The Great Joy" which "explodes silently upon the world" so that "no circumstance . . . is to be left out."[5] If we watch for it, we'll find this defiant joy in unexpected places.

While preaching in Belfast, Northern Ireland, I visited The Reverend Harold Good and his wife, Clodagh. Harold is a former president of the Methodist Church in Ireland who received the World Methodist Peace Award for helping negotiate the peace agreement ending the armed conflict in Northern Ireland. During "the troubles" Harold served as a pastor along the wall separating Catholic nationalists and Protestant loyalists. He provided pastoral care to people who experienced the worst of the violence that churned around them.

When people ask Harold about his role as a peacemaker, he laughs and says he was just a "tea maker." He says he invited people for tea, helped them listen to each other, and helped them take stumbling steps toward peace. I found Harold and Clodagh to be joy-saturated servants who were as delightful as Irish elves. Like them, we are commanded to be people of defiant joy.

Questions for Journaling

• When have you been hypnotized by the evil of this world?
• How have you experienced joy in unexpected places?
• What brings joy into your life? How can you share it with others?

Prayer

O God, I pray that your great joy will explode silently in my life. Let it flow through me as a defiant "nevertheless" in a world obsessed with evil and pain. Make me your agent of joy in everything I say or do this day. I pray in the name of the great joy-bringer, Jesus Christ my Lord. Amen.

Day 3: Living in Herod's World

Read Matthew 2:1-23.

W hat's Herod doing here? Why does Matthew give him a leading role in the Christmas drama? It's no wonder we'd rather
read Luke's version on Christmas Eve!

Matthew is a hard-core realist. As a tax collector, he has experienced the corruption of political and economic power. Matthew's Gospel draws a stark contrast between the kingdoms of this
world ruled by the likes of Herod or Pilate and the kingdom of God
revealed in Jesus. A persistent theme of Matthew's Gospel is that
we cannot serve two masters (see Matthew 6:24). The story forces
the choice upon us: Herod's way or Jesus' way? The kingdom of this
world's corrupted politics and self-serving power or the kingdom of
God's truth and self-giving love revealed in Christ?

Anyone who thinks the Bible is out of touch with the hard
realities of the "real world" should read Matthew. It's the up-to-date
account of the lengths to which insecure tyrants will go to protect
their power. Anyone who suggests that the church lives in an esoteric spiritual world that doesn't confront evil, suffering, and injustice should check out the liturgical calendar for December 28. Before
we've had time to pack away the Christmas decorations or finish the
leftover turkey, the church calls us to remember the Holy Innocents.

In the collect for December 28, we pray for God's mercy for
"all innocent victims." That means we are praying for a lot of people these days, from children separated from their parents on the
southern border of the United States to children who face starvation in war-torn countries around the globe. Then the collect asks

God to "frustrate the designs of evil tyrants and establish your rule of justice, love, and peace."[6] That means that we, as God's kingdom people, are called to be about the business of frustrating political tyrants and establishing justice, love, and peace in our world.

Matthew plants a word of hope in the story when he records, "After King Herod died . . ." (2:19). After Herod does his worst, he becomes little more than a calendar page to establish Jesus' birthday. And when Herod is gone, Jesus comes back. The promise is that although evil will have its day, God's justice, peace, and love ultimately will triumph over all the powers of injustice, evil, and death.

In times when I've been discouraged by the polarization of the world's politics, the lack of compassion in our culture, the apparent ineffectiveness of the church's witness, or the evidence of racial and economic injustice around us, I've returned to William Sloane Coffin's reminder that hope is "a state of mind independent of the state of the world. . . . It makes us persistent when we can't be optimistic, faithful when results elude us. . . . Hopeful people are always critical of the present but only because they hold such a bright view of the future."[7]

May we be committed to truth when falsehood infects our politics, to peace when the world is saturated with violence, to love when hate threatens to overwhelm us, and to hope when optimism fails, through Jesus Christ our triumphant Lord.

Questions for Journaling

- What makes you feel that you are living in Herod's world?
- How do you understand the difference between optimism and hope?
- What signs of hope do you see in your ministry?

Prayer

We remember today, O God, the slaughter of the holy innocents of Bethlehem by King Herod. Receive, we pray, into the arms of your mercy all innocent victims; and by your great might frustrate the designs of evil tyrants and establish your rule of justice, love, and peace; through Jesus Christ our Lord, who lives and reigns with you, in the unity of the Holy Spirit, one God, for ever and ever. Amen.[8]

Day 4: We Go Forward!

Read Mark 16:1-8.

First words matter. In the first words from the other side of death, the angel announces, "He isn't here. . . . He is going ahead of you into Galilee. You will see him there" (Mark 16:6-7). It's as if the angel is saying, "You'd better get moving! He's already ahead of you. You'll have to run to catch up." The women find the risen Christ not in the graveyard of the past but along the road that leads to the future.

Roland Rink often closed his reports on the work of Africa Upper Room Ministries with the hope-filled declaration "We go forward!" It reminded me that one of the sure signs of the presence of the risen Christ in our lives is that we are always going forward. Followers of the risen Lord are rooted in the past, but we don't live there. We follow the risen Christ into an often uncharted and unpredictable future. We live with the promise that the risen Lord goes before us through life, through death, into life everlasting.

That's not to say that going forward is easy. I'll bet there were plenty of times when the apostles wished they could go back or silently hoped they would not need to go any farther. But the way forward is always forward. A friend of mine likes to say that because of Easter, tomorrow is never just another day. The Resurrection means that God isn't finished with us or with this world. We are on our way toward the fulfillment of God's saving purpose for our lives and in the whole creation.

I'm glad that "We're Marching to Zion" is the final hymn in *The United Methodist Hymnal*. This energetic marching song filled with hope and joy is a musical way of saying that we never stop going forward. We are always on the way toward the fulfillment of God's kingdom promise. We're always marching to Zion.

Eugene H. Peterson wrote, "Ordinary time is not what biblical people endure or put up with or hurry through as we wait around for the end time and its rocket launch into eternity."[9] He pointed to the way "end time influences present, ordinary time, not by diminishing or denigrating it but by charging it, filling it with purpose and significance."[10]

The ordinary ministries we offer in the ordinary places where we serve are a present expression of the promise that the kingdoms of this world will in fact become the kingdom of our God, and Christ will reign forever. There are times when that promise is enough to energize us for a long and joyful obedience as we follow the risen Christ. We go forward!

Questions for Journaling

• How do the first words at the tomb make you feel?
• How can you encourage your congregants as they travel the uncharted and unpredictable journey of following Christ?
• What is your next step forward?

Prayer

Thy Holy Spirit lead us on
Until our glorious goal is won;
Eternal praise, eternal fame
Be offered, Savior, to thy name!

—Georg Weissel (1590–1635),
trans. Catherine Winkworth
(UMH, no. 213)

Day 5: Aim for Heaven

Read James 4:13-17; Matthew 24:36-51.

I was nine years old when *A Man Called Peter* was nominated for an Academy Award in 1956. It was the story of a young Presbyterian preacher named Peter Marshall who emigrated from Scotland and became the nationally recognized Chaplain of the United States Senate. That movie was one of the early experiences that planted the seeds of my calling to be a preacher.

One scene in the movie depicts the day Marshall preached in the United States Naval Academy chapel. On the way to Annapolis he felt led to change his sermon and took as his text, "For what is your life? It is even a vapour, that appeareth for a little time and then vanisheth away" (James 4:14, KJV). He reminded the young midshipmen of the tenuous nature of life, the reality of death, and the promise of eternal life. That was Sunday, December 7, 1941. No one knew that while the midshipmen were in worship, the Japanese were attacking Pearl Harbor. It was the last sermon many of them would hear before serving in a war from which many would not return.

Hugo Schmidt was in the chapel that day and never forgot Marshall's words. A picture-perfect representative of what Tom Brokaw named the "Greatest Generation," he served with distinction in the Navy, returned to Tampa where he met the woman with whom he shared seventy years of marriage, built a business, raised a family, and became a leader in the community. Simply put, he lived the faith.

No one loved his church more deeply or served more effectively than Hugo. He was faithful in worship, even when he had to watch the service by livestream from his bed. Every pastor who served Hyde Park United Methodist Church was blessed by his wisdom, laughter, and friendship. When he died at ninety-eight, we celebrated a life that demonstrated what Marshall preached in the Academy chapel. Hugo knew the tenuous nature of life, made the most of every day, and died in the hope of the resurrection. He requested that his memorial service include his favorite hymn, "Christ the Lord Is Risen Today." C. S. Lewis could have been describing Hugo when he wrote this: "The Christians who did most for the present world were just those who thought most of the next. . . . Aim for Heaven and you will get earth 'thrown in.'"[11]

I end this study with Hugo's story as a reminder that we serve in ordinary time with our eyes fixed on the extraordinary promise of resurrection. We live as faithful servants who are doing their Master's work, anticipating Christ's return and energized by the hope of life everlasting. There's nothing ordinary about that!

Questions for Journaling

• Who represents "The Greatest Generation" in your life?
• How do the reality of death and the hope of eternal life shape your ministry?
• What will it mean for you to be doing your Master's work when Christ comes?

Prayer

We pray to Thee, O Christ, to keep us under the spell of immortality. . . .

Let us more and more come to know Thee as a living Lord who hath promised to them that believe: "Because I live, ye shall live also."

Help us to remember that we are praying to the Conqueror of Death, that we may no longer be afraid nor be dismayed by the world's problems and threats, since Thou has overcome the world.

In Thy strong name, we ask for Thy living presence and Thy victorious power. Amen.

—Peter Marshall[12]

APPENDIX:
STEPS TOWARD HOLY FRIENDSHIP

In the first week of this study, I identified small group community as one source of power that sustains us for the long obedience of ministry, quoting E. Stanley Jones who called this kind of fellowship "a conspiracy of love" in which we are "unreservedly committed to Christ and unbreakably committed to each other." This kind of community is easier to describe than it is to develop.

Britt Gilmore, a Florida pastor serving at Knock Methodist Church in Belfast, Northern Ireland, gave me helpful feedback during the writing of this resource. He described the practical challenge of building this kind of community:

> I feel a need (and have for a long while) for a few holy friendships that might offer encouragement, honesty, and accountability, but I have found this difficult to nurture. Part of this is the busyness of life with ministry and family commitments. Part of it is my more introverted nature. Another part is because I have journeyed to a new continent and the relationships I did have in a "clergy covenant group" are faint with the strain of distance. Though clergy colleagues here are open and welcoming, many of them have long, rich relationships from living their whole lives on this island. I am open to these types of friendships but have found them challenging to nurture.

You don't have to move across the Atlantic to share Britt's experience. Like any human relationship, the "spiritual friendship" that St. Aelred described doesn't just happen. It moves beyond the typical level of relationships in classes or small groups to develop more intimate, long-term relationships. It is the result of intentional effort, a willingness to try and sometimes fail, and openness to Spirit-energized surprise. The question is, how does it happen? What are some practical steps toward this kind of Christian community?

In 1982, three young pastors in their first years of ministry felt a need to focus their attention on developing their spiritual discipline of prayer. I was only a few years ahead of them, but they asked me to lead them in a retreat at Jonathan Dickinson State Park in West Palm Beach, Florida. I pulled some books and resources off my shelves and headed south in an attempt to be their mentor in prayer. It didn't take long, however, to discover that I was in the same place they were. As we spent the time together, we found that we enjoyed being together. We learned from one another and went away with a desire to continue sharing our lives and ministries together.

A year later we met again for three days in a condominium on the Atlantic Ocean through the generous hospitality of one of our church members. We've continued meeting together twice a year for thirty-seven years. One by one, the group grew to ten as we found other pastors who shared the same need for reflection, friendship, relaxation, and fun. We've been through a lot together—challenges in pastoral appointments, drug and sexual abuse of children, divorce and remarriage, retirement, cancer, the death of parents. We know that we are better men and better pastors because of the depth of our relationships and expect to keep sharing these times together until we are sitting in rocking chairs on the nursing home porch. We're also grateful that the story of our group has spawned other small groups of clergy across our state, some of whom jokingly refer to us as "the Jedi Council."

Our experience provides a possible pattern for developing this kind of community.

- *Start small.* Jesus promised that wherever two or three of his disciples are together, he is with them. Find one or two other people and get together for coffee or lunch to see if there is the potential of a growing relationship.

• *Begin with friendship.* This kind of group doesn't work unless the people in it feel comfortable with one another and enjoy one another's presence. Begin by simply getting to know one another.

• *Find common goals.* Share with one another your own spiritual hunger and what you would hope to experience in a small group. John Wesley's "holy club" at Oxford was a response to a hunger for deeper faith and a life of holiness.

• *Develop a pattern.* In getting started, it helps to have a design for the time together. A guide for sharing is included here. My hope is that this book would be a beginning resource for groups like this.

• *Be ready to grow.* Watch for other colleagues who might fit into the group along the way.

• *Give grace to quit.* Not every attempt at this kind of community works over time. Be honest enough to acknowledge if the group is not accomplishing what you hoped it would and allow it to end.

• *Have fun!* Look for opportunities to do things you enjoy. A clergy covenant group that is younger and more athletic than ours runs a marathon together each year.

• *Be prepared for surprises.* Keep your eyes open for the unexpected things that the Holy Spirit might do in your lives through being together.

Britt concluded his comment with the good news that he had nurtured a friendship with a Presbyterian minister. They shared together in a retreat at a Benedictine monastic community that may be the start of a "conspiracy of love" for him.

A GUIDE FOR SMALL-GROUP GATHERINGS[1]

E xcept for his appearance to Mary on Easter morning (see Matthew 28:1-10), every appearance of the risen Christ happens when the disciples are together: breaking bread in Emmaus (see Luke 24:13-35), gathered in the upper room (see John 20:19-23), sharing breakfast on the beach (see John 21:1-14), and at the Ascension (see Matthew 28:16-20). The post-Resurrection stories indicate that although we may have our own individual experiences with Christ, it's more likely that we will know his presence in the presence of other disciples in worship, fellowship, and small-group sharing.

The purpose of small groups in this study is for each person to share what they have discovered in the scripture readings, written reflections, and personal prayer during the week. The role of the group leader is not to lecture or teach but to facilitate conversation. Here is a sample outline for small groups.

Gathering

- *Getting Acquainted.* In the first session, invite each person to share his or her name and one reason he or she chose to participate in the group.
- *Checking In.* Begin each week by sharing one new discovery made this week.
- *Opening Prayer.* The opening prayer can be offered by the leader or can rotate among the group members each week. It can be spontaneous or could be a traditional prayer from resources such as the Book of Common Prayer.

Discussion Questions

• What surprised or challenged you in the readings this week?
• Where did you find yourself in this week's material?
• Which scripture reading spoke most deeply to you?
• Share the next step each person will take to live into what they have learned.

Prayer

• Let each member express how they would like to be remembered in prayer.
• After a time of silence, go around the circle with each person either offering a word of prayer or simply passing to the next person.
• Close with everyone saying the Mizpah blessing from Genesis 31:49 (NRSV): "The LORD watch between you and me, when we are absent one from the other."

NOTES

Epigraph. William Law, in *Holy Women, Holy Men: Celebrating the Saints* (New York: Church Publishing, 2010), 318–19.

Introduction

1. Eugene H. Peterson, *Subversive Spirituality* (Grand Rapids, MI: Wm. B. Eerdmans Co., 1997), 260.
2. Richard Heitzenrater, *Diary of an Oxford Methodist Benjamin Ingham, 1733–1734* (Durham, NC: Duke University Press, 1985), 2.
3. Harry Emerson Fosdick, *The Manhood of the Master* (New York: Association Press, 1913), 155.
4. Jack Jackson, *Offering Christ: John Wesley's Evangelistic Vision* (Nashville, TN: Kingswood Books, 2017), 119.

Week 1: Power

Epigraph. David Brooks, *The Road to Character* (New York: Random House, 2015), 264–65.

1. Margaret W. Brown and Howard L. Brown, "Follow, I Will Follow Thee" (1935); https://hymnary.org/text/jesus_calls_me_i _must_follow.
2. Friedrich Nietzche, *Beyond Good and Evil*, trans. Helen Zimmern (Project Gutenberg, 2009), chap. V, par. 188. https://www.guten berg.org/files/4363/4363-h/4363-h.htm#link2HCH0005.
3. T. S. Eliot, "Ash Wednesday", *Modern American Poetry*, ed. Louis Untermeyer (New York: Harcourt, Brace & World, 1958), 401.
4. Eugene H. Peterson, *Under the Unpredictable Plant: An Exploration in Vocational Holiness* (Grand Rapids, MI: Wm. B. Eerdmans Co., 1992), 114–15.

5. Vida Dutton Scudder, *Holy Women, Holy Men: Celebrating the Saints* (New York: Church Publishing, 2010), 632.

6. Peter Marshall, *Prayers Offered by the Chaplain* (Washington, D.C.: Government Printing Office, 1949), 29.

7. Adapted from James A. Harnish, *Easter Earthquake: How Resurrection Shakes Our World* (Nashville, TN: Upper Room Books, 2017), 116–17.

8. James A. Harnish, *A Disciple's Heart: Growing in Love and Grace, Companion Reader* (Nashville, TN: Abingdon Press, 2015), 33.

9. Peter Storey, *I Beg to Differ: Ministry Amid the Teargas* (Cape Town: Tafelberg, 2018), 52.

10. E. Stanley Jones, *Is the Kingdom of God Realism?* (Nashville, TN: Abingdon Press, 1940), 203, 272.

11. E. Stanley Jones, *A Song of Ascents* (Nashville, TN: Abingdon Press, 1968), 48.

12. John Wesley, *The Works of John Wesley*, vol. XII (Grand Rapids, MI: Zondervan, 1872 reprint), 251.

13. Wesley, *The Works of John Wesley*, 252–53.

14. Wesley, *The Works of John Wesley*, 253.

15. Wesley, *The Works of John Wesley*, 254.

16. John Wesley, *The Works of John Wesley*, vol. XIII (Grand Rapids, MI: Zondervan, 1872 reprint), 13,

Week 2: People

Epigraph. Eugene H. Peterson, *Under the Unpredictable Plant: An Exploration in Vocational Holiness* (Grand Rapids, MI: Wm. B. Eerdmans Publishing Co., 1992), 62.

1. Charles M. Schulz, cited in Stephen J. Lind, *A Charlie Brown Religion: Exploring the Spiritual Life and Work of Charles M. Schulz* (Jackson, MS: University Press of Mississippi, 2015), 37.

2. James Weldon Johnson, "The Creation," *God's Trombones: Seven Negro Sermons in Verse*, ed. Henry Louis Gates Jr. (New York: The Viking Press, 1927; Penguin edition 2008), 15.

3. Henri J. M. Nouwen, *The Wounded Healer: Ministry in Contemporary Society* (Garden City, NY: Doubleday & Company, 1972), 63.

4. Charles Wesley, "Savior, the World's and Mine," *John & Charles Wesley: Selections from Their Writings and Hymns—Annotated and Explained*, Paul Wesley Chilcote (Woodstock, VT: Skylight Paths, 2011), 63.
5. Harry Emerson Fosdick, *A Book of Public Prayers* (New York: Harper & Brothers, 1959), 172.
6. Bob Merrill, "People," from *Funny Girl* (1964).
7. David Brooks, "A Nation of Weavers," *The New York Times*, February 18, 2019, https://www.nytimes.com/2019/02/18/opinion/culture-compassion.html.
8. Carole King, quoted in *Mojo Collection: The Ultimate Music Companion*, ed. Jim Irvin and Colin McLear (Edinburgh: MOJO Books, 2007), 229.
9. Scudder, *Holy Women, Holy Men*, 167.

Week 3: Place

Epigraph. Eugene H. Peterson, *Under the Unpredictable Plant: An Exploration in Vocational Holiness* (Grand Rapids, MI: Wm. B. Eerdmans, 1992), 130–31.

1. Richard Lischer, *The End of Words: The Language of Reconciliation in a Culture of Violence* (Grand Rapids, MI: Wm. B. Eerdmans Publishing Co., 2005), 33.
2. Robert Frost, "The Road Not Taken," www.poetryfoundation.org/poems/44272/the-road-not-taken.
3. Timothy B. Tyson, *Blood Done Sign My Name* (New York: Three Rivers Press/Random House, 2004), 288.
4. George Ella Lyon, "Where I'm From," http://www.georgeellalyon.com/where.html.
5. Joseph Addison, "When All Thy Mercies, O My God," Trinity Hymnal (1961), no. 51, https://hymnary.org/text/when_all_thy_mercies_o_my_god.
6. Frederick Buechner, *The Longing for Home: Recollections and Reflections* (San Francisco: HarperSanFrancisco, 1996), 2.
7. Peterson, *Under the Unpredictable Plant*, 122–23.

8. Donna Claycomb Sokol and L. Roger Owens, *A New Day in the City: Urban Church Revival* (Nashville, TN: Abingdon Press, 2017), 3.

9. Buechner, *The Longing for Home*, 2.

Week 4: Proclamation

Epigraph. James Baldwin, *James Baldwin: Collected Essays* (New York: Literary Classics of the United States, Inc., 1998), 306.

1. Lin-Manuel Miranda and Jeremy McCarter, *Hamilton: The Revolution* (New York: Grand Central Publishing, 2016), 59.

2. Miranda and McCarter, *Hamilton*, 59.

3. Miranda and McCarter, *Hamilton*, 59.

4. Robert Moats Miller, *How Shall They Hear Without a Preacher?: The Life of Ernest Fremont Tittle* (Chapel Hill, NC: University of North Carolina Press, 1971), 166–67.

5. Richard Lischer, *The End of Words: The Language of Reconciliation in a Culture of Violence* (Grand Rapids, MI: Wm. B. Eerdmans Publishing Co., 2005), 42.

6. W. H. H. Aitken, *The Oxford Book of Prayer*, ed. George Appleton (New York: Oxford University Press, 1985), 83.

7. Frederick Buechner, *Speak What We Feel (Not What We Ought to Say): Reflections on Literature and Faith* (New York: HarperCollins, 2001), ix.

8. E. Stanley Jones, *The Word Became Flesh* (Nashville, TN: Abingdon Press, 1963), 193.

9. Nickolas Butler, *Little Faith: A Novel* (New York: HarperCollins, 2019), 43–44.

10. Ron Rolheiser, quoted in Michael W. Higgins and Kevin Burns, *Genius Born of Anguish: The Life and Legacy of Henri Nouwen* (New York: Paulist Press, 2012), 69.

11. Henry Ward Beecher, in Debby Applegate, *The Most Famous Man in America: The Biography of Henry Ward Beecher* (New York: Three Leaves Press, 2006), 274. Quoted from William Beecher and Samuel Scoville, *A Biography of Rev. Henry Ward Beecher* (New York: Charles Webster, 1888).

12. Lin-Manuel Miranda, "It's Quiet Uptown" in *Hamilton: The Revolution* (New York: Grand Central, 2016), 253.

13. William Shakespeare, *King Lear*, Act 5, Scene 3.

14. Alan Paton, *Instrument of Thy Peace* (New York: The Seabury Press, 1968), 58–59.

Week 5: Perseverance

Epigraph. E. Stanley Jones, *The Word Became Flesh* (Nashville: Abingdon Press, 1963), 160.

1. Gil Rendle, *Quietly Courageous: Leading the Church in a Changing World* (Lanham, MD: Rowman & Littlefield, 2019), 21.

2. James Martin, SJ, "7 lessons for ministry I've learned as a Jesuit," *America: The Jesuit Review*, October 10, 2018, https://www.ameri camagazine.org/faith/2018/10/10/father-james-martin-7-lessons -ministry-ive-learned-jesuit.

3. Peter Storey, *I Beg to Differ: Ministry Amid the Teargas* (Cape Town: Tafelberg, 2018), 78–79.

4. T. S. Eliot, "Burnt Norton," *Modern American Poetry*, ed. Louis Untermeyer (New York: Harcourt, Brace & World, 1958), 404.

5. James Baldwin, *James Baldwin*, 333.

6. Archbishop Desmond Tutu, *Proceedings of the Fifteenth World Methodist Conference* (Waynesville, NC: World Methodist Council, 1987), 168.

7. Tutu, *Proceedings*, 169.

8. Tutu, *Proceedings*, 177.

9. Storey, *I Beg to Differ*, 8.

10. Peter Marshall, *Prayers Offered by the Chaplain of the Senate* (Washington, D.C.: Government Printing Office, 1949), 67.

11. Ginger Gaines-Cirelli, *Sacred Resistance: A Practical Guide to Christian Witness and Dissent* (Nashville: Abingdon Press, 2018), xx–xxi.

12. Gaines-Cirelli, *Sacred Resistance*, 42.

13. Storey, *I Beg to Differ*, 8.

14. Scudder, *Holy Women, Holy Men*, 591.

15. Andrew C. Lacy, "Sir Robert Shirley and the English Revolution in Leicestershire," https://www.le.ac.uk/lahs/downloads/1982-83/1982-3%20(58)%2025-35%20Lacy.pdf.

16. John Baillie, *A Diary of Private Prayer* (New York: Scribners, 1949), 113.

Week 6: Promise

Epigraph. Henri J. M. Nouwen, *The Wounded Healer: Ministry in Contemporary Society* (Garden City, NY: Doubleday & Company, 1972), 75.

1. Rendle, *Quietly Courageous*, 20–21.
2. Sam Keen, *Fire in the Belly: On Being a Man* (New York: Bantam Books, 1992), 171.
3. Keen, *Fire in the Belly*, 171.
4. Keen, *Fire in the Belly*, 171.
5. Thomas P. McDonnell, ed., *A Thomas Merton Reader* (New York: Image Books, 1989), 360.
6. *The Book of Common Prayer* (New York: Church Hymnal Corporation, 1977), 238.
7. William Sloane Coffin, *A Passion for the Possible: A Message to U.S. Churches* (Louisville, KY: Westminster John Knox, 1993), 3.
8. "The Lesson Appointed for Use on the Feast of Holy Innocents, December 28," https://www.lectionarypage.net/YearABC/HolyDays/HolyInno.html.
9. Eugene H. Peterson, *Christ Plays in Ten Thousand Places: A Conversation in Spiritual Theology* (Grand Rapids, MI: Wm. B. Eerdmans Publishing Co., 2005), 67.
10. Peterson, *Christ Plays in Ten Thousand Places*, 67.
11. C. S. Lewis, *Mere Christianity* (New York: Touchstone, 1996), 119.
12. Peter Marshall, *Mr. Jones, Meet the Master* (New York: Fleming H. Revell, 1949), 115.

A Guide for Small-Group Gatherings

1. Adapted from James A. Harnish, *Easter Earthquake: How Resurrection Shakes Our World* (Nashville, TN: Upper Room Books, 2017), 119–21.